THANK GOD IT'S MONDAY

If you are:

- someone who is thinking about changing your job or career
- a seriously unhappy employee
- an employer looking for ways to improve staff efficiency and morale
- a graduate in search of your first job
- an older person returning to the work force

this book is for you. It offers sound, practical advice that will help you understand your goals, and direct you toward the type of work environment most likely to meet them. Getting the right start in the right direction is a sure-fire way to guarantee a career filled with happiness.

As a consultant to several corporations in the fields of personnel and organization, and with over 30 years as an executive, LEONARD H. CHUSMIR has performed extensive research in the areas of motivation, personnel, and women in management. Author of over 50 scholarly articles and the book *Matching Individuals to Jobs*, Dr. Chusmir currently serves as Associate Professor of Management at Florida International University in Miami.

THANK GOD IT'S MONDAY
The Guide To A Happier Job

Leonard H. Chusmir, Ph.D.

A PLUME BOOK

NEW AMERICAN LIBRARY

A DIVISION OF PENGUIN BOOKS USA INC., NEW YORK
PUBLISHED IN CANADA BY
PENGUIN BOOKS CANADA LIMITED, MARKHAM. ONTARIO

NAL BOOKS ARE AVAILABLE AT QUANTITY DISCOUNTS WHEN USED
TO PROMOTE PRODUCTS OR SERVICES. FOR INFORMATION PLEASE
WRITE TO PREMIUM MARKETING DIVISION, NEW AMERICAN LI-
BRARY, 1633 BROADWAY, NEW YORK, NEW YORK 10019.

Published simultaneously in Canada by Penguin Books Canada Limited.

 PLUME TRADEMARK REG. U.S. PAT. OFF. AND FOREIGN COUNTRIES
REGISTERED TRADEMARK—MARCA REGISTRADA
HECHO EN DRESDEN, TN, U.S.A.

SIGNET, SIGNET CLASSIC, MENTOR, ONYX, PLUME, MERIDIAN
and NAL BOOKS are published in the United States by
New American Library, a division of Penguin Books USA Inc.,
1633 Broadway, New York, New York 10019,
in Canada by Penguin Books Canada Limited,
2801 John Street, Markham, Ontario L3R 1B4

Library of Congress Cataloging-in-Publication Data

Chusmir, Leonard H.
    Thank God it's Monday : a guide to a happier job / Leonard H.
Chusmir.
        p.   cm.
    ISBN 0-452-26374-3
    1. Job satisfaction. I. Title.
HF5549.5.J63C48   1990
650.14—dc20   89-13368
                                                           CIP

First Printing, February, 1990

    2   3   4   5   6   7   8   9

PRINTED IN THE UNITED STATES OF AMERICA

To my wife, Janet,
who has made every day a joy for me

Contents

Fulfill Needs for Achievement and Affiliation • Jobs
That Fulfill Needs for Affiliation and Power

Preface

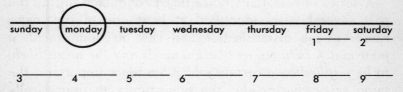

sunday	monday	tuesday	wednesday	thursday	friday	saturday
					1	2
3	4	5	6	7	8	9

We live in an era of increasing dependence on high technology, automated production, and financial belt-tightening. Our industries struggle to survive in global competitive battles with Western Europe and Japan, as well as Third and Fourth World countries in Southeast Asia, South America, and Africa.

Some writers blame American workers for our country's economic ills, contending that their work ethic consists of doing only what they must do and no more. That view is overly simplistic and incorrect. The work ethic is as strong as ever and may well be growing stronger.[1]

The paradox, however, is that the realization of that work ethic may be diminishing. Research shows that only 25 percent of American workers feel they are working up to their potential. Half claim they don't put much effort into their work and do only what they need to do to keep their jobs. More than half are dissatisfied at work; most readily admit they could be much more effective.

If Americans have a strong work ethic but a weak productivity record, obviously something is wrong. Something is preventing them from doing their best. We must identify the cause.

A series of research studies that I conducted during the past several years identified at least one of the major causes of job dissatisfaction and lack of commitment: *a poor match between motivation needs and the needs likely to be fulfilled by a certain job.* Even more important, the same research provides the opportunity to dramatically reduce the discrepancy between work ethic and work productivity.

Happiness, productivity, and fulfillment at work do not take an act of Congress or a heavenly miracle. Happiness at work is within reach of every worker, within reach of every reader.

This book may change your life. It is written especially for:

- *Persons who are unhappy at work but are not sure why.* You will learn how to find out if your job matches your needs and what to do to become one of the fortunate minority who are so happy at work they look forward to Monday mornings.
- *Persons trying to decide on a long-term career path.* By listing possible promotions on your way up, you can tell which jobs will be satisfying and which will be frustrating.
- *Persons in fields where job opportunities are narrowing because of mergers, competition, new products.* By checking the list of jobs that match your needs, you can redirect your efforts to promising new jobs and careers.
- *Students who must decide on a college major.* By matching your motivation profile with the appropriate job, you can choose the career that will make you happy, rather than the career that might get you a quick job out of college but long-term discontent.

- *Women who want to return to the work force.* The skills you learned while running your household and managing your family may easily be applied to any number of "just-right" jobs listed in this book.
  —Leonard H. Chusmir, Ph.D.

NOTES

1. Daniel Yankelovich and John Immerwahr, "Management and the Work Ethic," in James L. Gibson, John M. Ivancevich, and James H. Donnelly, Jr. eds., *Organizations Close-Up: A Book of Readings*, 5th ed. (Plano, TX: Business Publications, 1985), pp. 388–395.

1 Thank God It's Friday

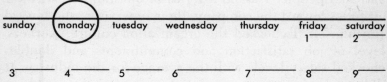

sunday	monday	tuesday	wednesday	thursday	friday	saturday
					1	2
3	4	5	6	7	8	9

When I first met Jim and Sally Ferguson they had been married for nineteen years. They and their two teenage children lived in a quiet, well-manicured Denver suburb. Jim ran his own accounting firm. Sally, who began her career when the children started school, was a computer programmer for a large manufacturing firm.

Jim telephoned me at the university one afternoon. One of the M.B.A. students in my organizational behavior class worked for Jim. It was he who recommended that Jim contact me. Jim wanted me to do some consulting work for his accounting firm. A medium-sized organization that had been very profitable, it was starting to lose its effectiveness—and a few of its best clients. Several key employees had quit during the year; morale in the office had slipped badly.

We met at his office and talked. Jim explained that no matter how hard he seemed to work—he was now putting in six full days a week and several evenings—the office was falling further behind. It wasn't a question of being shorthanded. Quite the opposite. He had two more accountants on the payroll this year than last, despite a drop in revenue. Jim told me he was desperate. "Can you help me out?" he asked. I agreed to take the job. It took me a couple of days to interview most of Jim's key professional and staff people. I asked a series of questions about their attitudes toward the company, their supervisor, and toward Jim himself. I checked the organization culture, workers' level of job satisfaction and commitment, and double-checked salary levels with the average for the industry. It didn't take long to figure out the cause of the problem: Jim. A brilliant accountant and tax expert, he often was short-tempered, intolerant of human error, difficult to talk to and reluctant to let his key people handle clients without looking over their shoulders and second-guessing their decisions.

At lunch one day, as we discussed my interview results, Jim admitted he was very unhappy with himself, and with his life.

He wasn't sure why. He felt like a failure. What started out to be a promising, successful career had deteriorated into a daily struggle. Relationships at home weren't too great, either. At the rate things were going, his marriage was heading for trouble too.

"I'd like to meet your family," I said. "Maybe together we can figure out what's causing some of this unhappiness." I had no idea whether his work, home life, or both were the source of his behavior. Certainly something was creating a serious problem. We needed to find out quickly.

A week or so later, as the family and I chatted after dinner in the living room, the picture became much clearer. The Fergusons loved their life and enjoyed the status and comforts their combined incomes brought. They looked forward to Fridays when they could escape from their miserable week at work. It took most of Saturday for them to unwind. By Saturday night they usually felt pretty relaxed. Unfortunately, by late Sunday afternoon, both Jim and Sally were uptight again as they anticipated Monday morning and the start of another week of frustrating and unfulfilling jobs.

Jim had wanted to be a tax accountant since his first introductory accounting course in college. He visualized himself trying to figure out how to save a client's money on taxes, or competing against an IRS agent in a dispute over deductions. The image propelled him into a bachelor of science in accounting, a master's in accounting, and soon after graduation, certification as a certified public accountant. For the first five years after college, Jim worked for one of the Big Eight firms, specializing in tax work.

Eventually, Jim went into practice for himself. He opened his office with just a secretary and a part-time accountant, and the practice prospered. Before long, Jim was making a very fine living. He was never happier. He had a great job, a wonderful, loving wife, and two terrific kids. Work started to be a drag, Jim said, when he had to hire several accountants to help him cope with the rapidly expanding practice. Instead of having fun doing the kind of work he had always dreamed of doing, he spent more than half the day supervising other accountants. The more the business grew, the more time he spent managing, until eventually he did almost no hands-on work. He didn't mind working sixty or seventy hours a week. The profits rolled in. Then, just when things looked brightest, Jim's practice started its downward spiral.

Jim and Sally were brought up to believe that the man earned the living and the woman stayed home to care for the family. As the children grew older and less dependent on Sally, however, she too wanted a career. She read the employment ads for computer programmers and was impressed with the money that career offered. She didn't know what was involved in computer work, but was assured by several friends that it was a perfect match. She was good at math; it was the type of work you could do part-time in case working full-time and caring for the children was too much. Sally went back to school for technical training and landed a job almost immediately. She was very good at her work. During the first couple of years, she received several raises and was given more important programs to design and implement.

Sally confessed that at first she was very happy and proud of what she was able to accomplish. But little by little, with Jim working so many long hours and the children spending more time with their friends, she felt isolated. As a computer programmer, she worked alone all day solving problems. Although her work was challenging and paid very well, she wished she could be like so many others in the company who worked with people they enjoyed and who seemed to be having so much fun. When she would come home from work and find a note that Jim would be late, she would resent being left alone.

The resentment built up, slowly but steadily. Sally couldn't bring herself to complain. Jim was working so hard and was so tense that he'd probably snap her head off anyway. She didn't want to fight, and she didn't want to feel guilty. Most of all, she didn't know what to do to escape this misery. Sally knew she ought to be happy. Instead, life was empty. Jim not only was unhappy, he was in danger of losing his business. It was sad to think that these years that should have been—could have been— joyful and fulfilling were so stress-filled and unhappy.

I thought I knew how to help Jim and Sally.

"I think I have an answer to the problem," I told them that night. "If I'm right, Jim can save his practice and Sally can be happy at work again. Soon, maybe you'll thank God it's Monday instead of Friday.

"I want you take this little test," I told them.

2 How to Determine Your Motivation Needs

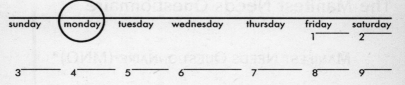

sunday	monday	tuesday	wednesday	thursday	friday	saturday
					1	2
3	4	5	6	7	8	9

The test I asked Jim and Sally to take is the "Manifest Needs Questionnaire." It only has fifteen short questions and was developed by two well-known and highly respected researchers, Richard Steers and Daniel Braunstein. It is a valid and reliable measure of motivational needs—those drives that push people toward behaviors and actions that will help satisfy and fulfill their needs. The test has been used in research hundreds of times in the past decade.

"Here's how you take the test," I told Jim and Sally. "Don't take too long to answer each of the questions. It's most accurate when you mark down the first answer that comes to mind. There are no 'right' or 'wrong' answers. The more you think about the 'right' answer, the more likely you'll only kid yourself. Since it's your career and job at stake, be sure to answer all the questions frankly."

They both took the test. If you're one of fifty-four million Americans who are unhappy at work, who—if they had it to do all over again—would not pick the same job,

you ought to take the test too.[1] Follow the same directions
I gave to Jim and Sally Ferguson. It's your first step
toward becoming happier at work.

The Manifest Needs Questionnaire

MANIFEST NEEDS QUESTIONNAIRE (MNQ)*

Instructions. Below are fifteen listed statements that
describe things people do or try to do on their jobs. We
would like to know which of these statements you feel
most accurately describe your own behavior when you are
at work. Please place a check in the box next to that word
which best describes your own actions. Remember: there
are no right or wrong answers. Please answer all questions
frankly.

1. I do my best when my job assignments are fairly difficult.
   - ☐ *always*
   - ☐ *almost always*
   - ☐ *usually*
   - ☐ *sometimes*
   - ☐ *seldom*
   - ☐ *almost never*
   - ☐ *never*

2. When I have a choice, I try to work in a group instead of by myself.
   - ☐ *always*
   - ☐ *almost always*
   - ☐ *usually*
   - ☐ *sometimes*
   - ☐ *seldom*
   - ☐ *almost never*
   - ☐ *never*

*Adapted from: Richard M. Steers and Daniel N. Braunstein, "A
Behaviorally-Based Measure of Manifest Needs in Work Settings," *Journal of Vocational Behavior*, vol. 9 (1976), pp. 251–266. Reprinted with
permission.

3. I seek an active role in the leadership of a group.
   - ☐ *always*
   - ☐ *almost always*
   - ☐ *usually*
   - ☐ *sometimes*
   - ☐ *seldom*
   - ☐ *almost never*
   - ☐ *never*

4. I try very hard to improve on my past performance at work.
   - ☐ *always*
   - ☐ *almost always*
   - ☐ *usually*
   - ☐ *sometimes*
   - ☐ *seldom*
   - ☐ *almost never*
   - ☐ *never*

5. I pay a good deal of attention to the feelings of others at work.
   - ☐ *always*
   - ☐ *almost always*
   - ☐ *usually*
   - ☐ *sometimes*
   - ☐ *seldom*
   - ☐ *almost never*
   - ☐ *never*

6. I avoid trying to influence those around me to see things my way.
   - ☐ *always*
   - ☐ *almost always*
   - ☐ *usually*
   - ☐ *sometimes*
   - ☐ *seldom*
   - ☐ *almost never*
   - ☐ *never*

7. I take moderate risks and stick my neck out to get ahead at work.
   - ☐ *always*
   - ☐ *almost always*
   - ☐ *usually*
   - ☐ *sometimes*
   - ☐ *seldom*
   - ☐ *almost never*
   - ☐ *never*

8. I prefer to do my own work and let others do theirs.
   - ☐ *always*
   - ☐ *almost always*
   - ☐ *usually*
   - ☐ *sometimes*
   - ☐ *seldom*
   - ☐ *almost never*
   - ☐ *never*

9. I find myself organizing and directing the activities of others.
   □ always
   □ almost always
   □ usually
   □ sometimes
   □ seldom
   □ almost never
   □ never

10. I try to avoid any added responsibilities on my job.
    □ always
    □ almost always
    □ usually
    □ sometimes
    □ seldom
    □ almost never
    □ never

11. I express my disagreements with others openly.
    □ always
    □ almost always
    □ usually
    □ sometimes
    □ seldom
    □ almost never
    □ never

12. I strive to gain more control over the events around me at work.
    □ always
    □ almost always
    □ usually
    □ sometimes
    □ seldom
    □ almost never
    □ never

13. I try to perform better than my coworkers.
    □ always
    □ almost always
    □ usually
    □ sometimes
    □ seldom
    □ almost never
    □ never

14. I find myself talking to those around me about non–business-related matters.
    □ always
    □ almost always
    □ usually
    □ sometimes
    □ seldom
    □ almost never
    □ never

15. I strive to be "in com-
    mand" when I am work-
    ing in a group.
    ☐ *always*
    ☐ *almost always*
    ☐ *usually*
    ☐ *sometimes*
    ☐ *seldom*
    ☐ *almost never*
    ☐ *never*

Scoring Key for Manifest Needs Questionnaire (MNQ)

Step 1. Questions, 6, 8, 10 and 11: Score 1-2-3-4-5-6-7 in that order for the descriptions checked under each question. Mark the score to the left of the question number.

Step 2. All other questions: Score 7-6-5-4-3-2-1 in that order for the descriptions checked under each question. Mark the score to the left of the question number.

Step 3. Fill in the blank spaces below with scores for each of the fifteen questions.

Achievement items: 1. _____
                                        4. _____
                                        7. _____   TOTAL: _____
                                      10. _____
                                      13. _____

Affiliation items:

2.	_____
5.	_____
8.	_____ TOTAL:_____
11.	_____
14.	_____

Power items:

3.	_____
6.	_____
9.	_____ TOTAL:_____
12.	_____
15.	_____

NOTE: Use the following scales to convert raw motivation scores to low, medium, or high levels of each need. Norms are based on scores of 800 individuals in research by Leonard Chusmir and cover a broad range of people at all hierarchical levels.

	Need for Achievement	Need for Affiliation	Need for Power
Low (lower ⅓) Up to:	25	18	20
Medium (middle ⅓)	26–28	19–20	21–23
High (upper ⅓) More than:	29	21	24

Scoring the Manifest Needs Questionnaire

When Jim and Sally finished taking the test, I asked them to score the questionnaire using the *scoring key* printed just after the last question. *Please do the same.* Your score for each of the three needs will range from 5 to 35, but more than likely your score will be somewhere between 15 and 30.

Next, look at the norms at the very bottom of the questionnaire. Those are the scores of about eight hundred working people.

- If your score for any one need falls in the lowest one-third of the norms, call that a "low" need.
- If your score for any one need falls in the middle one-third of the norms, call that a "medium" need.
- If your score for any one need falls in the highest one-third of the norms, call that a "high" need.

Jim had a score of 30 in need for achievement, 16 in need for affiliation, and 20 in need for power. Comparing him to the norms, I told Jim that his 30 in need for achievement was high; the 16 he scored in need for affiliation was low; and his 20 in need for power also was low. His dominant need, therefore, is the need for achievement.

Sally's need-for-achievement score was only 22, which is low; her need-for-affiliation score was 26. That's high. Her need-for-power score of 19 also is low. Her dominate need, therefore, is affiliation.

What was your score? Fill in the blank spaces below:

My score for *need for achievement* is _____. That means that my need for achievement is:

	☐ Low
(check one)	☐ Medium
	☐ High

My score for *need for affiliation* is ————. That means that my need for affiliation is:

(check one)
- ☐ Low
- ☐ Medium
- ☐ High

My score for *need for power* is ————. That means that my need for power is:

(check one)
- ☐ Low
- ☐ Medium
- ☐ High

I explained to Jim that even though his affiliation score is 16 and his power score is 20, his need for power is not higher than his need for affiliation. This may be confusing to people, but raw scores on two separate scales are not usually related to each other—only to other raw scores on the same scale. It's important to remember that your numerical score is not used for anything other than to see whether that score is high, medium, or low compared to other workers throughout the country.

Very often, two needs are tied, with either two high scores or two medium scores. In that case, the person is said to have a combination of specific needs. Sometimes all three needs are tied. They may all be high or medium or low. That person has a balanced motivation profile. Remember that you do *not* have to score in the high category for that need to be dominant or "highest." It is dominant if it is in a higher category than any other need, regardless of the category.

When we measure needs using paper and pencil tests such as the "Manifest Needs Questionnaire," our answers are based on how we feel about ourselves at the time the test is given. *Manifest* needs are those that are plainly visible and on the surface at the time we take a motivation test. Other, more complicated tests measure our *latent* needs—those not so visible and more permanently part of our personality. Unfortunately, those types of tests require trained psychologists to interpret and score, so they're rarely used in the work world. Most often our answers to the Manifest Needs test reflect our true motivation needs, but once in a while we may experience an event so major in our lives that it could trigger a response that is temporarily different from our normal need. For example, if we recently divorced, or lost a loved one, our need for love or belonging (need for affiliation) might be temporarily high. If we were just fired from our job, it's possible that our need for achievement might be affected in the same way for a short time. If your score is unexpectedly different from what you think it might normally be, ask yourself if there has been a major change during the past few days or weeks that could be affecting the outcome of the test. If so, modify your score accordingly.

What Is *Your* Dominant Need Profile?

There are seven possible dominant motivation profiles that may be fulfilled at work.
They are:

- Need for achievement
- Need for affiliation
- Need for power
- Balanced needs
- Needs for achievement and power
- Needs for achievement and affiliation
- Needs for affiliation and power

As you'll remember, I told Jim that his dominant motivation need profile is the need for achievement. Sally's is the need for affiliation.

Which of the seven possible motivation profiles do you have?

My dominant motivation need profile is: _____.

(fill in)

What the Fergusons' Test Scores Revealed

Jim's and Sally's test results confirmed my original impression that both of them had needs that were not being fulfilled at work.

Jim has a high need for achievement. My research proved that this need *used to be* fulfilled when he did hands-on tax accounting but was no longer being fulfilled by managing other people. That job fulfills the need for power. No wonder Jim was miserable at work! His needs were not being fulfilled. Sally, too, was badly matched with her job. Her dominant need is affiliation. Yet her work mostly fulfilled achievement needs! No wonder she was frustrated and unhappy at her computer programmer position.

Later, I'll explain what it means to fulfill needs, how specific jobs fulfill specific needs, and exactly how I was able to help Jim and Sally Ferguson become much happier at work. How happy? So happy they look forward to Monday mornings instead of dreading them.

How About You?

If you had to do it all over again, would you pick the same job?

Wouldn't it be wonderful, for a change, to look forward to Monday instead of Friday? To look forward to the beginning of another work week and not the end of it? Wouldn't it be wonderful to be excited about your job? Wouldn't it be wonderful to be up for the challenge, to be enthusiastic about your colleagues, happy about the time spent at work? There are many people who feel that way. They don't have aches in their stomachs. Sunday night, they look forward to going to work. You can too. All you have to do is read on. The answers are here, in this book.

Be sure to remember what *your* motivation profile is. After you read the next few chapters, you'll understand all you need to know to be satisfied, fulfilled, and truly happy at work.

NOTES

1. Edward E. Lawler III, "Satisfaction and Behavior," in Richard M. Steers and Lyman W. Porter, eds., *Motivation and Work Behavior*, 3rd ed. (New York: McGraw-Hill, 1983), p. 338.

3 What Makes People Happy at Work

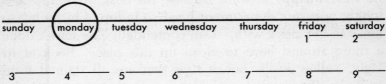

Happiness at work often helps bring happiness at home. The reverse, unfortunately, is also true. Jim and Sally Ferguson are a perfect example. Unhappy at work, it was affecting their marriage. Unhappiness at work *usually* affects our personal lives. It's almost impossible to leave discontent behind, like a pen in a desk drawer, when we go home.

People give many reasons for being unhappy at work. They say:

- The pay is no good.
- The boss is crummy.
- The work is too tough.
- The work is too easy.
- The work is too boring.
- The job offers no security.
- The job offers little chance for advancement.
- The company doesn't give a damn about me or the other workers.
- The company just cares about making money.

We've all heard these and other explanations from those who dislike their jobs. Many of us also have used some of these excuses.

Dan, a twenty-six-year-old shipping clerk, was convinced he was unhappy at work because his boss, Arthur, was a tough, uncaring department head. "On top of his being so lousy to get along with," Dan contended, "he hasn't done a thing around here to clean up this place. Look at it. Ugly, yellow walls; bench tops that are all stained from spilled coffee; sealing tape dispensers that were antiques when my old man came over from Italy before I was born." Dan's friend Sammy, who works alongside Dan, said he didn't care about "the color of the walls, or any of that stuff. As far as I'm concerned," Sammy complained, "there's no way I can get ahead around here. And I'll be damned if I want to be a shipping clerk for the rest of my life."

Both Dan and Sammy were unhappy at work, but for different reasons. Studies that focus on the major sources of dissatisfaction show that the most common reasons have to do with pay, promotion, security, leadership, and the work itself. Sometimes it's difficult to figure out which specific problem triggers unhappiness in a specific person. Some may react to poor leadership, others are frustrated by poor pay or the lack of security. Still others react to a combination of things. The problem is that understanding what makes people *unhappy* at work can be quite complicated.

Happy Jobs

Understanding what makes people *happy* at work used to be just as complex. But recent research provides the information that can lead to more happiness and fulfillment on the job. That same research can help you look forward to Monday mornings.

The research shows that if a person is "properly fitted" to the job—in other words, if a person's needs match the job—there probably will be someone who is satisfied with the job, committed to the job. As a result the person won't call in sick as much, will be less likely to leave the job, and will produce work of a higher quality. These add up to pretty good goals for everyone—employees, employers, managers, companies. For the individual it means a happy work life. For the company it means higher profits.

Let's look at a neighbor of mine, Len, who has been with the same wood-working shop for ten years. He loves his job because he was brought up to believe that when you use your hands to create something beautiful, you will leave a piece of yourself on earth after you die. "I know a lot of people with much more money who work all day and have nothing but a paycheck to show for it," he said. "Take this cabinet I'm working on. A hundred years from now it'll still be here, maybe even more beautiful than today as it ages. Someone can say, 'Isn't it wonderful? Len Slavik the cabinetmaker made it. See his signature on the back?' " Len has a high need for achievement. He always wants to do something better and better. His job fulfills that need, and Len is very happy at work.

Fitting People to Jobs

There are different ways of fitting people to their jobs.

One way of fitting a person to the job is to find out if the person *can* do the job. In other words, is he or she *capable* of doing the job if he or she *wants* to do it? That's fairly easy to find out. In some cases, hiring managers check a job applicant's references (which may be a little dangerous—no one submits a bad reference); some managers may depend on degree qualifications.

A Florida engineering firm I consulted for used to hire students with B.S. degrees in engineering right on the spot when the recruiter attended the yearly college placement fair. When engineers were tough to get, the recruiter assumed the student would be a good fit for the job. All too often, however, the match was awful. College graduates sometimes have a poor idea of what real-world jobs involve. They usually have the technical skills needed for entry-level engineering jobs, but that doesn't mean they have other skills, such as the ability to get along with coworkers or clients. Also, depending on the school students attend, their ability to communicate orally and in writing may not be adequate. So, after a half-dozen graduates didn't work out, the firm asked me what to do. They took my advice, stopped relying on degree qualifications, and added testing to the hiring procedures.

Most companies test job candidates for verbal and math ability, motor and sensory skills, and job knowledge. There are also tests that businesses may choose to use to determine if someone is aggressive or passive, has good social skills, and so on. All of these ability, job knowledge, or personality tests tell us whether the person has the necessary skills and *can do* the job that needs to be done.

But what good is it if the person *can do* the job but either doesn't want to or is miserable while doing it? The answer, of course, is that it's *no* good. They'll do the job for a while, but within two to five years (at best), most will either quit or be fired.[1] What can be even worse is that the person may spend a longer time at the job being miserable. Everyone doesn't leave.

Unfortunately, many people believe that if they're good at a job, if they have the technical skills or ability to do it, they'll be happy. That isn't true. Most of us can learn any skill we want, if we try hard enough. We might be terrific at cooking, but we wouldn't want to be a chef. We might be perfectly capable of typing, but we wouldn't want to be a secretary. We might be good at driving, but we wouldn't want to be a taxi driver.

Sometimes students go to school to earn a degree in a subject they think will land them a good-paying job. They end up with a job that does indeed pay well or offer advancement and security. But it doesn't fulfill their other needs.

Sally Ferguson, as you probably remember, did exactly that. When the children started first grade, Sally went to school to become a computer programmer. It caused several years of unhappiness and nearly cost her her marriage.

Sometimes young people pursue a profession or career because their parents pushed them in that direction. Our graduate schools of business are filled with full-time working students attending classes at night, trying to get M.B.A. degrees because they're unhappy engineers, nurses, teachers, or other kinds of professionals. Their parents may be happy, but the students are miserable in jobs that fulfill their parents' needs, not their own.

Job or school counselors also may mislead people seeking advice. These counselors often use tests designed to tell a person's vocational "interests." Of course, interests are important, just as ability and skills are important. But there's often a big chasm between interest in a particular occupation and fulfillment from it.

One of my friends, Roberto, when he was seventeen and a college freshman, went to the counseling department. They gave him the Strong-Campbell Interest Inventory, which is a very fine test to determine what vocation a person would be interested in. It turned out that one of Roberto's great leanings was toward art, and at the counselor's suggestion, he majored in applied fine arts during his four years. The Strong-Campbell test is quite accurate, and Roberto did very well learning the technical end of the art profession. Unfortunately, he struggled for several years as an artist who was technically good but unfulfilled by his work. It might have made a great hobby for him, but not a great career. Eventually, Roberto found an ideal compromise. He started his own import-export business specializing in art objects. As I told him, "The job of artist fulfills the need for achievement. Your need for achievement is moderate, but your need for power is very high. Running your own art business fulfilled both needs."

New Research

From research conducted over more than two years, we now know that:

A job that fulfills a person's motivation needs is likely to be a job that brings happiness.

We now know that if we can determine a person's needs and what particular needs a job fulfills, we can tell if there's a good match between the person and the job. If the match is very good, the person is likely to be happy at work. If it's very bad, the person is likely to be unhappy at work. If the match is somewhere between very good and very bad, there are steps that can be taken to increase the degree of happiness and job satisfaction.

How to Be the Right Person for the Right Job

Most people don't have to be told whether they're happy or unhappy at work. You know it as well as you know your own name. You don't have to take a psychologist's test to find out that you're miserable. It doesn't take a genius to figure out that you hate your job if you "Thank God it's Friday" at the end of every week and wake up on Monday morning dreading going to work.

If you're happy at work, wonderful. Continue doing what you've always done and don't mess around by changing jobs, unless of course, it's a promotion. If you're unhappy at work, it's very important to find out why. You may be able to do something about it. Unfortunately, it's not always easy to figure out *why* you're unhappy. Organizational behavior researchers know that people often blame unhappiness on things they think are the reasons, such as poor pay, a bad boss, not enough time off, and so on. It's difficult for people to understand that the cause of unhappiness usually can be traced to a poor fit between motivation needs and the needs that are fulfilled by the job.

Hiring the Right Person for the Right Job

If you are in a position to make hiring or promotion decisions, you need to make sure that you do everything you can to hire people whose needs are a good match for their jobs. It is cheaper and much more practical to fit the individual to the job than to change the job to fit the individual. Also, as mentioned earlier, people whose needs are not satisfied by the job will end up frustrated and angry and either will keep quitting their jobs, do such poor work that they're fired, or suffer physical and/or emotional consequences that will continue until they find something that *is* satisfying—something they're suited for motivationally.

Turnover is very expensive. Every nonmanagerial person who quits or is fired costs the average United States organization between three and four thousand dollars in severance pay, benefits, and recruiting and training his or her replacement. When it comes to replacing a major person—let's say a middle- to high-level manager—the average cost skyrockets to about ten times the person's monthly salary. This adds up to about twenty to one hundred thousand dollars *per manager* in turnover costs.[2]

For example, John was forty-seven years old when he got a telephone call from a client of mine, a major producer of electronic products in Boulder, Colorado. The company chief executive officer told John that they had recently lost their head of production and asked if John would be interested in leaving his present employer in northern Oregon. "I might be," John told the CEO, "if it's worthwhile financially and if I don't have to spend any money because of the move. Aren't houses very expensive in Boulder?" John asked. "And what are mortgage rates now? We have a 6 percent mortgage on our present house." John eventually was offered the job and accepted. His new employer guaranteed the sale of his Oregon home; kept up the payments until it was sold; absorbed all legal and real estate commission costs for the old house and mortgage costs and points for the new house. He also gave John a cash bonus to make up for the difference in home costs and mortgage rates (new mortgages in Boulder were then 10 percent compared to the 6 percent John had been paying); gave another cash bonus to pay for redecorating the new house; reimbursed him for moving van expenses; and paid for several trips to Boulder for John's wife to find a job and a house. Including what the electronics firm had to pay the old head of production in severance pay, repurchase of stock options, and other miscellaneous fringe benefits, the turnover cost the company more than $140,000.

John's predecessor, the old head of production, had worked for the company for several years. He was allowed

to "resign" after a series of minor personality problems
became major. The CEO thought the old production head
was going through some kind of mid-life crisis, but at the
exit interview I learned it had nothing to do with his
personal life. As the factory became automated, he was
bored with his job and found it unfulfilling. Had management realized this as soon as the problems began, it might
have been able to help solve the problem.

It's very important, then, to understand which needs a
job fulfills. By measuring the actual needs of the job
candidate (using the motivation need test in Chapter 2), you
can make sure that the applicant has needs that match or
are similar to those that will be fulfilled by the job. A good
fit is a major key to a stable and satisfied work force. When
jobs are matched to needs, your employees enjoy their jobs
more, have stronger motivation, stay on the job longer,
and are not absent as much.[3] The company's effectiveness
is increased by the higher levels of satisfaction and job
performance.[4] Operating costs are substantially lower because of the ensuing reduction in turnover and absenteeism.

When considering whom to hire or promote, you should
use matching information as an additional diagnostic
device—not as the only factor. When motivation testing is
used along with tests and measures designed to find out if
a candidate can perform the work, interviews, and application forms, legal or fairness problems are unlikely.

Promoting the Right Person to the Wrong Job

We've all seen what happens when people good at one
job are promoted to another job for which they're not
suited. Managers usually find out *after* they've promoted
them, when it's too late to save them.

A salesman, Bill, had worked for his construction products wholesaler for eight years. I was told that he was terrific, and a fine professional—their very best. He was so competitive that most often he closed the sale and beat the competition. When an opening came up for the sales manager's job, there just was no question—Bill got the job.

But everyone soon realized that a terrible mistake had been made. Bill had been a good sales rep. But, as a sales manager, his people skills were awful. The other sales reps hated him because he picked on everyone and said he could have done a better job. A perfectionist who couldn't understand that other people were only human, Bill was arrogant, didn't delegate responsibility, was a "loner," tended to be authoritarian in leadership style, and didn't get along well with people in the community. A number of sales reps quit; they claimed they had better opportunities elsewhere, but a few admitted they couldn't stand the working conditions.

What the personnel director, or department head, didn't understand was that the newly promoted salesperson had a high need for achievement—great for most sales jobs, but terrible for management where a person supervises others and where good people skills are absolutely necessary. As we've already seen, the job of a manager fulfills, and requires, a high need for power. Bill had a high need for achievement, so the promotion to sales manager was a mismatch. *If* the personnel director, or whoever did the promoting, had tested Bill's motivation needs *before* the promotion, the procedure would have shown there was probably going to be a mismatch. The promotion was *management's* mistake, but Bill was fired for something over which he really had no control.

This type of mismatch should be avoided for all the obvious reasons. First is the human toll. It's very difficult to demote a manager—it rarely works out for anyone. Firing is an extreme and hurtful measure, which leaves egos and careers damaged. And it costs the organization much in time, money, and morale because of the turnover and reaction of all who know about it. The organization ends up with a whopping personnel and dollar drain.

How to Help "Bad Fits"

What can be done if someone's not really motivationally suited for a job? Sometimes, management development sessions help. Managers can be taught better people skills, better delegating skills. Sensitivity training, too, is often successful in helping managers see their subordinates in a different light and themselves the way others see them.

Very large companies usually have experts on the payroll to conduct in-house training sessions. But even those firms without salaried trainers often hire outside consultants or free-lance professionals to come into the company to teach key workers important self-help skills such as assertiveness training, stress reduction, conflict management, motivation, time management, and so on.

Most Americans, though, work for small- or medium-sized companies that don't possess the financial means to offer free self-help training to employees who are not well matched to their jobs. But there's still a lot that individuals can do to help themselves at little or no cost.

Courses are offered at junior colleges and universities throughout the country that help "fit" people to their jobs by teaching them the disadvantages and advantages, the problems and opportunities, the discomforts and joys of working alone or with others. These courses are usually referred to in college catalogs as "Organizational Behavior," and they're very helpful in identifying areas that need improvement.

You can help yourself, however, even without taking special courses or going through company training programs.

Now that you've taken and scored the Manifest Needs Questionnaire in Chapter 2, you already know which of your motivation needs are high and which are low. If your job fulfills one or more of your low needs, it would be very helpful if you could increase the strength of that need. A very successful way to do that is through *visualization*. Concentrate on seeing yourself doing the type of activity you normally dislike. At the same time, visualize other people applauding you or complimenting you on how well you're doing this activity. By visualizing very pleasant results, you will increase your enjoyment and eventually score higher in this type of fulfillment. Another effective tool to increase the satisfaction from doing something you normally don't enjoy is through self-given *rewards*. Whenever you do something at work that is unpleasant but necessary, give yourself a reward. The reward might be something like an ice cream cone, dinner out, a relaxing few minutes at home sipping a glass of wine as you unwind, a warm bath, or a facial or massage. In other words, do something nice for yourself as a reward. Eventually, this positive reinforcement will help make these activities more enjoyable and more automatic.

NOTES

1. David G. Winter, *The Power Motive* (New York: The Free Press, 1973).
2. Edward E. Lawler III, *Motivation in Work Organizations* (Monterey, CA: Wadsworth, 1973); Leonard H. Chusmir, *Matching Individuals to Jobs: A Motivational Answer for*

Personnel and Counseling Professionals (New York: AMA-COM, a division of the American Management Association, 1985).

3. J. Richard Hackman and Lawler, "Employee Reactions to Job Characteristics," *Journal of Applied Psychology*, vol. 55 (1971), pp. 259–286; David A. Nadler, J. Richard Hackman, and Lawler, *Managing Organizational Behavior* (New York: Little, Brown, 1979), chap. 3; Ronald R. Sims, "Assessing Competencies in Experiential Learning Theory: A Person-Job Congruence Model of Effectiveness in Professional Careers," Ph.D. dissertation, Case Western Reserve University, 1981.

4. Chusmir, "Male-Oriented vs. Balance-as-to-Sex Thematic Apperception Tests," *Journal of Personality Assessment*, vol. 47 (1983), pp. 29–35.

4 The Mystery of Motivation

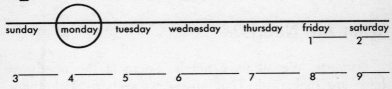

sunday	monday	tuesday	wednesday	thursday	friday	saturday
					1	2
3	4	5	6	7	8	9

Did you ever notice how people do things, sometimes, which just don't make sense? Did you ever wonder why?

The owner of a large retail furniture store, Larry admits that his employees drive him crazy. " Half the time I wonder if I'm the caretaker of a loony-bin instead of the owner of a store." Now forty-three, Larry used to get very upset when his salespeople or office staffers fought among themselves, left early for a night football game, or played practical jokes. His employees haven't stopped doing "strange" things, but Larry has felt much better since he hired a professional store manager to look after the help while he concentrated on the store's buying and promotion activities. He can't figure out why his store manager seems to accept all these shenanigans as "normal," but as long as he doesn't have to worry about it anymore, and the store makes a good profit, Larry's happy.

Many times people do things that don't make sense because something is pushing them. A motive. A need. Think how terrific it would be to understand these motives and needs and help people satisfy them. If you are a manager, you could watch your employees blossom into happy, productive workers. If you don't supervise others at work, understanding your own needs could help you become much happier, both on the job and at home.

What Are Needs?

Primary. We all have needs. Some of the needs we have are biological. That means we're born with them, and they're easy to recognize. We get hungry and thirsty. We have the need for food and liquid. We get cold and tired. We need warmth, shelter, sleep. We need oxygen. We need sexual release. The drive to satisfy these needs is as strong as our will to survive. That's why they're called primary needs.

Secondary. There are other needs, which are learned. They are not biological or physiological. They are psychological. They are needs that we develop as we grow older and experience life. Since we all have different experiences, these needs vary. They cover such areas as the need for security, the desire for comfort, the yearning to love or be loved, and the quest for status and achievement. There are other such needs. All of these, because they are learned, are called secondary needs.

The case of a colleague of mine at the university's business school provides an example. John had just earned his Ph.D. when he started teaching finance, and was an excellent researcher as well as knowing how to handle himself in the classroom. Our students were used to professors who wore long-sleeve shirts and ties—after all, they were teaching business courses and thought they should look like business people. But John always dressed in a three-piece, vested suit (pinstripes, naturally). His shirts were white-on-white, had French cuffs connected by solid gold links, and were initialed. When he stepped out of his Mercedes in the parking lot, he looked fancier than the president of the local bank. John had grown up in a very poor neighborhood near downtown Chicago. He told me once that he "was a street kid who never forgot what it was like to feel like a 'nothing.' I really can't afford it," he admitted, "but the clothes and car are very important to me." John, of course, had acquired a very high need for status and esteem.

Since we all come from such different backgrounds and have lived such different and varied lives, the secondary needs, or learned needs, are particularly complicated and varied. Just about anything managers do affects the secondary needs, so it's easy to see why a manager's job takes great sensitivity and understanding. When we work alongside other people, either as their peers or their subordinates, it's important that we try to understand their needs—as well as our own.

It would be easier if secondary needs were out on the top of the desk like a calendar, easy to see. But secondary needs often are hidden. Sometimes they're even hidden from their owners, who may not know what they are. Since secondary needs are hidden or disguised, one researcher contends that dissatisfied workers usually blame their dissatisfaction on something tangible that's easier to pinpoint than their own secondary needs.[1] He suggests that it would be easier for a worker who is not motivated to blame salary than to search deep inside and identify the secondary need that isn't being fulfilled. At any rate, it's important to remember that many disputes, such as wage disputes, may not be what they seem to be. Even when the requested raise is granted, it may not eliminate the underlying unrecognized and unexpressed dissatisfaction.

What Is Motivation?

Think of an engine that drives a piece of machinery and you've got the concept of motivation. Motivation is the force that moves people. Needs at the most uncomplicated level are the prime movers. They create a powerful force that makes people do many things.

For our purposes at work, let's remember that: *motivation* is simply the amount of *job-related effort* a person expends.

By way of example, David was a highly motivated person, competitive, and driven to achieve goals he had set when he was a teenager. Now thirty years old, David has climbed every fourteen-thousand-foot mountain in Colorado. He works out at the gym several days a week, is a fine golfer and a good friend to his many buddies. Unfortunately, David hasn't been able to keep a good-paying job. At work, his bosses believed David wasn't motivated. What they didn't understand was that he was strongly motivated, but not toward job-related effort. The challenge—still unmet—was to direct some of David's motivation energy toward accomplishing the types of goals needed for job success.

The amount of effort is determined mostly by how much that effort, or behavior, satisfies the person's needs. So, to understand motivation, ask yourself two important questions:

1. What needs move most workers?
2. How do workers determine how much energy they'll spend?

The answer to the first question is critical for everyone—nonmanager or manager. The answer to the second question is especially important for managers, since only they are in a position to act on the information.

All Working People Are Not Alike

No two people are alike. It's important to remember that. Our fingerprints are unique and so are our personalities and motivation profiles.

You Don't Have to Memorize a Bunch of Theories

If you've ever attended a motivation workshop or training session, then you know there are all sorts of theories about motivation. If you were doing scholarly research, it would be important to remember all of them. But you need to pay attention only to the two questions we posed earlier: (1) What needs move most workers? (2) How do workers determine how much energy they'll spend? The answers to those questions are what you need to know.

What Needs Move Most Workers?

During my years as a newspaper executive, I used to attend the national conferences of the Suburban Newspaper Association. One year, in the mid-1970s, I attended a workshop on motivation put on by an organizational behavior college professor from the University of Iowa. He started the workshop by asking the publishers what they thought motivated most of their workers. Almost unanimously, the publishers responded "money, pay, fringe benefits." "Okay," the professor said, "now tell us what motivates you." One by one the publishers reported that they were motivated by needs such as self-fulfillment, self-actualization, self-respect, and so on.

The publishers failed to realize that their workers—like people everywhere—were motivated by many of the same needs as the bosses. Even though their employees made less money than they did, the workers still earned enough to satisfy their basic, lower-level needs. What they were looking for—just like most of the publishers—was something to satisfy their higher-level needs.

Whether we're male or female, we are driven by what we are searching for rather than what we've found.[2] We all have the same needs. But because of our different experiences and society-assigned roles, some of our needs may be stronger or weaker than others' needs.

Lower-Level Needs Don't Motivate Most Workers

American workers' needs for the basic necessities of life are reasonably well satisfied. There may be some exceptions, but in most of the U.S. usually even the smallest paycheck will help meet physiological or lower-level needs. Minimum wages earned in all but the most expensive metropolitan areas put food on the table and buy enough clothing and shelter to keep warm. All of these will be modest; possibly shelter and clothing will be shabby, but they will satisfy the need for survival or physiological needs. Most jobs also provide moderately safe working conditions, decent fringe benefits, and fairly good job security.

While these things are important, they are usually not important enough to drive most people to work harder. Those basic, primary needs are no longer motivators to most U.S. workers. They're what Frederick Herzberg called "dissatisfiers" rather than motivators.[3] If we don't get a decent salary and other fringe benefits, we may be unhappy or dissatisfied. But getting them won't motivate most of us.

Exceptions are likely to be persons over forty. That group is more concerned with job security, working condi-

tions, and fringe benefits. Older workers are particularly
attracted by good pensions; it's easy to understand why.
Studies show that younger workers have little interest in
security-related benefits. Because most managers and owners of business are older, they tend to give fringe benefits
to their employees that the managers would like, but
younger employees don't care much about.

A generous boss, Sam had a very profitable year. He
decided to reward his employees, who were greatly responsible for the success of the company. He increased
pensions by more than 25 percent. Only two of his employees thanked him. Sam was amazed and very disappointed. The two grateful employees were fifty-seven and
fifty-nine years old. Most of the other workers were in
their early twenties. Their retirement was forty to forty-
five years away and had no real meaning. Things like extra
vacation time, free trips, or paid-up membership in a
health or social club would have meant much more to
them.

Higher-Level Needs Do Motivate Most Workers

In addition to working to make money, many people
work to fulfill higher-level drives. Sometimes they are
motivated by the need for identity or for personal fulfillment.

Many people have a *need to be liked*. They have high
needs for approval, belonging, and friendship. They have
a strong need to be accepted and to feel part of the group.
They want to be reassured; they want to know they are
valued and loved. They're often open and responsive.
They want friends. They may dislike working in an office
by themselves. An executive secretary, for example, may
be happier in a common reception room with other execu-

tive secretaries where he or she feels part of a group than alone in an office.

Other people may have a *need to feel worthwhile*. Their self-worth may be tied to someone else. They are someone's son, daughter, husband, wife, or employee. They have lower self-esteem and self-confidence than people who idertify with their own ego and talents. This is particularly *'.ae of some homemakers and recently divorced individuals. But some professionals suffer milder forms of the same lack of esteem. They're likely to be strongly motivated by their unfilled esteem and ego needs. They will respond to recognition as persons of worth.

When Bob's sales manager announced the new contest for salesperson of the month, Bob didn't think it was such a great idea. But, when he learned he was the winner of the first month's contest, he walked over to the bulletin board and saw the poster prominently displaying his picture, a headline "Salesperson of the Month," and the fact that he had sold more automobiles during June than anyone else—Bob was very excited and very pleased. He felt *important* and *valuable*.

Generally, most professionals have fairly good self-esteem. They view themselves as competent, productive, and worthwhile. Their work gives them psychological security, social status, and self-worth. Their ego needs are well satisfied.

The majority of people have a *need to be self-fulfilled*. This is particularly true of many professionals and managers who were brought up to believe that personal growth and achievement come from being competent at work. They find that self-fulfillment comes from a creative, challenging job. Like the publishers attending the newspaper conference, Kenny also had a need for self-fulfillment and thoroughly enjoyed his job as assistant to the publisher of a large weekly newspaper group. The pay was pretty good, but best of all his boss gave him interesting projects to take care of, and he was learning very fast. Some day he was sure he'd be a publisher too, and when his boss asked Kenny if he'd like to attend the conference this year, Kenny jumped at the opportunity.

All of these needs—to survive, to be secure, to be liked, to be worthwhile, and to be self-fulfilled—intuitively make sense and are popular in self-help books and organizational development training programs. Although there's little argument that these needs exist, most professional research experts have turned to another need theory. It is simpler to apply and has passed the test of time in terms of its ability to predict worker behavior.

A Very Useful Motivation Theory Easy to Apply to Happiness on the Job

In the 1940s, psychologist David McClelland and his colleagues developed a motivation theory that recognized three major needs particularly important to people at work.[4] During the next twenty years, research by McClelland and others verified and elaborated on the original studies. Tests were developed to measure each of the three needs accurately. Much is now known about how to apply those needs to work situations.

The three needs are:

Need for achievement. This is the need to compete against some standard of excellence, to do better and better, and to accomplish worthwhile goals.

People who are high in the need for achievement:

- Seek and assume a lot of personal responsibility
- Take medium calculated risks
- Set challenging but realistic goals for themselves

- Develop comprehensive plans to help achieve their goals
- Solicit and use specific and measurable feedback on the outcome of their actions
- Seek opportunities where their desire to achieve won't be thwarted

My client, tax accountant Jim Ferguson, had a high need for achievement. He used to fulfill it when he took responsibility for solving the tax problems of his clients by planning how they could save taxes. His feedback came as soon as he saw their yearly tax returns and realized how much money he had saved them. When his job changed and he had to spend so much time supervising others, his opportunity to achieve was thwarted. That's when Jim started to become very unhappy at work.

Need for affiliation. This is the need for close interpersonal relationships and friendship with other people. Also, social acceptance.

People who are high in the need for affiliation:

- Seek warm relationships and friendships
- Are not so concerned with getting ahead (like achievement needers), but enjoy jobs that provide interaction with people
- Prefer to work on committees with people they like rather than with experts
- Exhibit empathy and understanding
- Exhibit the need to help others and solve their problems

Jim Ferguson's wife, Sally, had a high need for affiliation. She wanted all the same relationships as those listed above. Unfortunately, even though she was technically very skilled in her work as a computer programmer, that job didn't fulfill many of her needs. Despite her programming ability and success, Sally was miserable.

Need for power. This is the desire to have impact and influence over other people. Ideally, the need is not to dominate. Instead, the individual puts the organization or society first and tries to make sure his or her leadership is just and fair.

People who are high in the need for power:

- Enjoy jobs where authority and power rest within their position
- Strive to be leaders
- Enjoy speaking assertively
- Enjoy personal recognition and approval

Unlike Jim Ferguson, Cynthia was a perfect fit to her job. Even though she was only twenty-eight years old, Cynthia commanded the respect and admiration of the thirty-five people who worked under her in the hospital medical lab. As head of the department, she had lots of opportunities for impact and influence over other people. One of Cynthia's greatest joys was seeing her employees develop the skills they needed to get the work out quickly yet at the level of quality demanded by the hospital. She enjoyed being leader of the lab and appreciated the personal recognition and approval she got from her subordinates, colleagues, and bosses.

Motivation Information Important for Managers

Most of us work for other people—about 87 percent of the nation's work force are nonmanagers. We can do a great deal to satisfy our own needs by making sure we pick the right job, but we have very little control over how much energy we'll spend to satisfy those needs. Managers have that responsibility. Therefore, the answer to the question how do workers determine how much energy they'll spend will be of interest mostly to managers.

Managers, of course, need to know their own motivation needs as well as those of their employees. According to McClelland, the best bosses have this motivation need pattern:

- Moderately high need for achievement
- Very high need for power
- Low need for affiliation[5]

That assumes, of course, that they have the other technical skills required to do the job.

Managers Also Need to Know How Workers Determine How Much Energy They'll Spend

Once we know a person's needs, we know what needs that person hopes to satisfy. But how hard will they try to satisfy their needs? The answer is that people will spend lots of energy on work if they get answers they *like* to these three questions:

1. What's in it for me?
2. Am I being treated fairly?
3. Do they recognize how hard I work?[6]

What's In It For Me?

Workers must be convinced that if they do what managers ask, they'll receive a reward that has value to *them*. It's important to remember that the worker's perception of value may be different from the manager's. Employees will be motivated to push hard at work when they believe that these three *sequential* steps will take place:

- A sincere effort will lead to accomplishing the job.
- Success will lead to the reward they expect.
- The reward will have real meaning and value to them.[7]

Peter was an executive M.B.A. student of mine when I taught organizational behavior at the University of Colorado at Denver. He was in charge of the structural engineering division of a large Denver architectural firm. The firm had a deadline to meet on plans for a high school, and Peter was having a little trouble getting his staff motivated. Two weeks after I lectured on expectancy theory (a fancy name for the question "What's in it for me?"), Peter telephoned me, all excited. "After I heard your talk, I thought I'd try the theory out at work," Peter told me. "I still can't believe the turnaround! I called a meeting the morning after class and I did the three steps you suggested. First, I gave the whole group a pep talk about how I knew that they had so much talent they could easily get this job done well before the deadline if they made the effort. Then, I promised that if we did get the job out on time, I'd make sure that they'd all get a long weekend off with pay and that the firm would pick up the tab on a skiing weekend for all of us at Vail. I knew that'd have real meaning and value to them, because we had been talking about doing something like that for a long time, but none of us could afford to take the time off from work.

It's critical that a person's expectations be supported. This means that there should be raises and promotions equal to effort. The reward that has most meaning and value to workers is satisfaction of their needs. Another valued reward is a good self-image. Managers must commit themselves to giving employees positive feedback in order to strengthen and nurture their subordinates' view of themselves. To be fully motivated, people must be convinced they're capable of success and that their effort will lead to effective performance.

Supervisors and managers can help this process by:

- Providing training programs to help employees develop the necessary skills to use their abilities *and*
- Clarifying performance goals for employees

Am I Being Treated Fairly?

Dorothy is the office manager for a distributor of painting supplies. A consultant had installed a standard plan for office-position evaluation. In setting up the plan, the keypunch operator's job was evaluated as one grade higher than that of a billing clerk, and as a result, Jenny, the keypunch operator, had received a seven-dollar-a-week raise to bring her up to the minimum rate for that position. Recently, one of the billing clerks, Sylvia, complained to Dorothy about her pay scale. "I'm almost always facing a backlog of my work. And it gets increasingly complicated. And I've been watching Jenny's work. She has plenty of time to spend in the lounge. And the stuff she handles is all routine. If she's worth seven dollars more a week, so am I."

Managers need to concentrate on equalizing pay. When they can't, other rewards valued by workers must be increased to compensate. These may include alternative work schedules such as flextime or four-day work weeks, opportunity for advancement, selection for training and development programs, recognition, and praise.

Do They Recognize How Hard I Work?

Recognize workers' efforts with the positive reinforcement of rewards.[8] Bosses should follow a four-step approach:

- Evaluate each employee in terms of desired work behavior.
- Identify practices that need strengthening.
- Work with each employee to clarify and establish new behavioral goals.
- Reinforce observed desirable behavior *as it takes place*.

At his exit interview, Ben told the personnel director that he finally had to quit because his new supervisor never said a word to him when he did a good job. "I spoke to him a couple of times," Ben complained, "but all he told me was that if I didn't hear from him that'd mean everything was okay. But my old boss, Carl, was terrific. He always made me feel good and all it ever took was a 'thanks' and a pat on the shoulder. This new guy is a cold fish," Ben said. "I can't work here anymore."

Rewards may include praise, recognition, a pay raise, a simple "Nice job!" or any other reward you recognize as being important to the worker. Remember, employees have to begin somewhere in making improvements. Reward them for any effort they make in the right direction.

Do Motivation Needs Change?

Motivation needs are an important part of a person's personality. Because needs are learned as we experience and react to events in our lives, they may change as our experiences change. But the process is very slow. It takes years rather than weeks or months. One of the major characteristics of personality is that it wants to be consistent. For that reason, human beings have an inborn tendency to resist change. Once our needs become part of our personality, they will be with us for a long time.

Age and those events related to age do make a difference, however. For example, boys are encouraged more than girls to participate in competitive sports, helping them develop a need for achievement at an early age. Young girls traditionally are encouraged to value relationships rather than competition, increasing their need for affiliation. As both genders get older and attain success, their need for achievement drops while their need for power increases.

NOTES

1. Keith Davis, *Human Behavior at Work* (New York: McGraw-Hill, 1986).
2. Abraham H. Maslow, *Motivation and Personality*, 2nd ed. (New York: Harper and Row, 1970); Maslow, "A Theory of Human Motivation," *Psychological Review*, vol. 50 (1943), pp. 370–396.
3. Frederick Herzberg, Bernard Mausner, and Barbara Synderman, *The Motivation to Work* (New York: John Wiley, 1959); Herzberg, *Work and the Nature of Man* (Cleveland: World, 1966).

4. David C. McClelland, *The Achieving Society* (Princeton, NJ: Van Nostrand, 1961); McClelland, *Human Motivation* (Glenview, IL: Scott, Foresman, 1985).
5. McClelland and David H. Burnham, "Power Is the Great Motivator," *Harvard Business Review*, vol. 54 (March–April 1976), pp. 100–110.
6. Andrew J. Dubrin, *Human Relations*: A Job Oriented Approach, (Reston, VA: Reston Publishing 1981), pp. 96–97.
7. Victor H. Vroom, *Work and Motivation* (New York: John Wiley, 1964); Lyman W. Porter and Edward E. Lawler III, *Managerial Attitudes and Performance* (Homewood, IL: The Dorsey Press and Richard D. Irwin, 1968).
8. B. F. Skinner, *Science and Human Behavior* (New York: Macmillan, 1953); Skinner, *Contingencies of Reinforcement* (New York: Appleton-Century-Crofts, 1969).

5 Jobs to Fulfill Your Needs

Early Need Fulfillment Research

Since the 1950s and 1960s, when McClelland and his colleagues developed and refined the motivation theory that identified the three basic needs of achievement, affiliation, and power, a few researchers have tried to link one or more of the needs with specific occupations. Each attempt involved testing a large group of people in one type of job to see what dominant need the majority of those tested possessed. There was some early success. For example, it was discovered that high need for achievement was commonly found among attorneys, entrepreneurs, physicians, research scientists,[1] salespersons,[2] chemical engineers and architects,[3] and management trainees.[4] Nurses and special education and residential teachers scored high in need for affiliation,[5] as did bartenders[6] and customer service representatives.[7] High need for power was linked to social workers, psychologists, psychiatrists,[8] insurance executives, middle-level personnel males, and college professors.[9]

New Research on Which This Book Is Based

It was not until the mid-1980s, however, that a more serious effort was made to develop a way of identifying the needs likely to be fulfilled by all twenty-two thousand job types in the United States, rather than just the few on the preceding list. Using a methodology called content analysis, I examined the written job descriptions of thousands of jobs. I combined that analysis with a U.S. government rating of the functions—with data, people, and things—workers perform on each job. By combining the two analyses, I developed a system that identifies how much need for achievement, need for affiliation, and need for power each job is likely to fulfill. Over the next two years, I performed nine different research projects to test the new system and to confirm its accuracy.[10]

Since I completed my original research and wrote the book explaining the concept to personnel, guidance, and counseling professionals, two other researchers have tested my job-match model using data gathered from incumbents of nine different jobs.[11] They deliberately used a different measure of needs for achievement, affiliation, and power to see if the theory would hold up with another, independent test. Information was obtained by testing 302 men and women deputy sheriffs, senior executives, middle managers, ministers, nurses, nursing supervisors, supervisors of engineers and scientists, technical people, and vending machine operators. In every one of the nine job categories, they confirmed the accuracy of the dominant need predictions. In more detailed analyses looking at the relative strength of all three needs in each of the nine jobs, their research supported twenty-one of the twenty-seven motive comparisons made. The probability of this happening by chance is less than one percent. Other, more complicated data analysis also confirmed the overall accuracy of my original research.

Nearly five hundred of the most popular occupations and jobs taken from the larger study are listed in the Appendix. There are lists of jobs for each of the seven need groups.

Increase Your Chance for Happiness on the Job

Now that you know what your basic needs are, and which are the strongest, it is time to figure out which jobs are most likely to satisfy those needs. In short, which jobs are a good match with *your* specific motivation need profile?

Whether you're a student, a newcomer to the job market, a woman returning to the work force, a person who is unhappy in a current job, or someone trying to plan a long-term career move, if the job you're thinking about is listed under the "matching" heading, go ahead with your plans. If you have or can learn the necessary skills, you probably will enjoy that job very much.

If it—or a similar job—is not listed, think seriously before you commit yourself to that position or career. It is quite likely that you will feel frustrated and unfulfilled by your choice. You probably will not want to stay with that job beyond two to five years at best. At worst, you may end up fired because it will be so difficult to be motivated to do your best.

Remember: Jobs that fulfill a person's needs are jobs that add up to happiness at work. If you want to wake up on Monday morning glad to go to work again at a job you find exciting and satisfying, find the section in the Appendix that lists jobs that match your profile.

Even though you are unhappy in your present job and now realize—after checking the job lists in the Appendix—that your position is a mismatch in terms of need fulfillment, you still may not want to give up your job. For many workers, changing jobs is very difficult. Economic times may be bad and new jobs difficult to find. Or, you may not be able or willing to take the chance of leaving your present job. Perhaps the pay is exceptionally good, or there are personal circumstances that make it difficult to switch.

Read to the end of each of the next five chapters for dozens of good ideas about how to be happier at work without changing jobs.

NOTES

1. David C. McClelland, *The Achieving Society* (Princeton, NJ: Van Nostrand, 1961).
2. McClelland and David H. Burnham, "Power Is the Great Motivator," *Harvard Business Review*, vol. 54 (March-April 1976), pp. 100–110.
3. J. B. Ritchie and Paul Thompson, *Organization and People [Instructor's Manual]* (St. Paul, MN: West, 1980), p. 110.
4. J. D. W. Andrews, "The Achievement Motive and Advancement in Two Types of Organizations," *Journal of Personality and Social Psychology*, vol. 6 (1976), pp. 163–168.
5. J. Clayton Lafferty, *Level 1: Life Styles Interpretation Manual* (Plymouth, MA: Human Synergistics, 1980), p. 13.
6. Ritchie and Thompson, *Organization and People*.
7. John R. Schermerhorn, Jr., James G. Hunt, and Richard N. Osborn, *Managing Organization Behavior* (New York: John Wiley, 1982).

8. David G. Winter, *The Power Motive* (New York: The Free Press, 1973).
9. Lafferty, *Level 1: Life Styles*, p. 11.
10. Leonard H. Chusmir, *Matching Individuals to Jobs: A Motivational Answer for Personnel and Counseling Professionals* (New York: AMACOM, a division of the American Mangement Association, 1985).
11. John W. Medcof and Michael J. Stahl, "Job-Motive Compatibility: A Test of a Model," unpublished paper, McMaster University, Faculty of Business, Hamilton, Ontario, Canada, L8S 4M4.

6 Achievement: The Drive That Energized America's Entrepreneurial Spirit

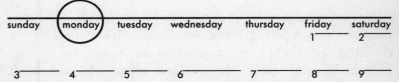

sunday	monday	tuesday	wednesday	thursday	friday	saturday
					1	2
3	4	5	6	7	8	9

David McClelland, father of the Need for Achievement theory, originally defined this profile as the "need for success in competition with some standard of excellence."[1] Years later he described it more generally as simply the pleasure derived from doing something better than it was done before.

If the need for achievement is your dominant need, you're about to learn a great deal about yourself and many people like you. Everything written here may not apply, but most of it will.

Remember, there is nothing "good" or "bad" about any motivation need profile. Your profile simply shows what you want satisfied in order to be happy at work and at home. A "good" motivation profile for one job or career may be "bad" for another. If your motivation profile is "bad" for your present job, don't worry. This chapter will explain what type of jobs would be "perfect" for satisfying *your* motivation needs. Or, if you don't want to change your job to one with a better motivation fit, you'll find lots of good suggestions for making life at work a lot easier and happier.

Need for Achievement and Economic Success

Need for achievement is said to be responsible for the rise of the world's greatest economic civilizations. It is credited with being the inspiration for America's vibrant entrepreneurial spirit, the attitude about life and work that took the United States from an agricultural society to an industrial power in less than one hundred years. McClelland found numerous examples of high need for achievement among the ancient Greeks as early as 520 B.C. In the succeeding centuries, those societies that valued achievement rose to great power and economic success. From reading the literature of the country, researchers revealed that increases in the achievement aspirations and behavior of those cultures were consistently followed by increased economic development. Nations and cultures with less achievement orientation fell far behind. One of the great and most prosperous civilizations of the Renaissance, Florence, flourished and then died. McClelland offered this explanation in *The Achieving Society*:

> The Florentines lost interest in achievement. Their dreams changed. They became more concerned with love and friendship, with art, with power struggles. The

dominant Medici family illustrates the shift in motivation from Giovanni, the great merchant banker whose
achievement drive led him to all corners of Europe,
through Cosimo, *pater patriae*, who consolidated his
father's gains, through Lorenzo, *Il Magnifico*, great pa-
tron of the arts, to his successors caught in a bloody
struggle for pleasure, power and wealth for their own
sake. What each generation wanted above all, it got.
What saves such a statement from banality is the new
fact that the psychologist has now developed tools for
finding out what a generation wants, better than it
knows itself, and *before* it has had a chance of showing
by its actions what it was after. With such knowledge
man may be in a better position to shape his destiny.[2]

Childhood Sources of Need for Achievement

Psychologists are convinced that there are meaningful
differences in need for achievement by the time children
reach the age of five. Mothers play a particularly strong
role in their sons' acquisition of need for achievement
between the ages of eight and ten. Parents of sons with
high need for achievement tend to expect more from their
children. Those parents show more warmth and affection
than parents of sons with low need for achievement. Mothers of the high-achievement boys tend to be more authoritarian; they give more specific directions than mothers of
the low-achievement boys. The reverse is true of the
fathers. Fathers of high achievers were less authoritarian
than those of low achievers. It's clear that domineering
mothers did not negatively affect the achievement need,
but that domineering fathers did. Fathers who encouraged
independence, who allowed their sons to proceed on their

own and to learn from their own mistakes, tended to raise high-need-for-achievement boys. The amount of independence given boys by their mothers does not appear to have substantial impact.

There are no published studies to date on sources of need for achievement for girls, so no one is sure if the same relationships would apply.

Three Behaviors Typical of Need for Achievement

According to the original method used by McClelland and his colleagues to score this need, people were said to have a high need for achievement when they were concerned and involved with one or more of the following three situations.[3]

Competition with a standard of excellence. High-need achievers enjoy competitive activity rather than pure aggression, where winning or doing as well or better than someone else is the primary concern. They're generally concerned with how well they're performing a particular job, regardless of how well someone else is doing. For example, a student winning an essay contest or an apprentice wanting to show the master machinist that he too can fix the machine are typical. Often the standard of excellence involves not competition with others but rather meeting self-imposed requirements of good performance. The person may be concerned with doing a good, thorough job.

Edward was a brilliant engineer in his early thirties who needed almost no supervision. What little he got he resented. "I've never cared what anyone else thought about my work," he confessed. "I'm good at what I do, and I always design my jobs so they'll withstand much more stress than called for by the building code. The trick is to incorporate the higher standards without adding to the cost of the project."

Unique accomplishment. High-need achievers are interested in accomplishing tasks that go beyond the ordinary, run-of-the-mill daily routine. They want to accomplish something that will mark them as a personal success. Inventions, artistic creations, and other extraordinary accomplishments are good examples.

I once asked a friend—sixty-eight years old—why he continued starting new businesses. "You don't need the money—you're already a millionaire ten times over. Why don't you retire and relax? You deserve it." Dave laughed. "You're right, Len," he told me. "But I just can't help it. If this new product works like we think it will, it'll revolutionize the health-care business. I just can't resist it."

Long-term involvement. High-need achievers are tenacious. They stick to their goals for years at a time. They have a clear idea of what they want to accomplish, and they keep at it until they do it. Even though the goal may be years off or take great personal sacrifice, they will stay with it. Personal success is critical. People whose goals involve becoming machinists, doctors, lawyers, or successful businesspersons are examples of those with long-term career involvement.

Gretchen was a reporter I knew years ago when I was in the newspaper business. Forty years old, she was a junior in college. She had been attending the University of Miami for six years, part-time at night after finishing her job at the newspaper. She told me she was going to be a lawyer, specializing in libel law, because she enjoyed the law and it would be a terrific combination with her journalism experience. I didn't want to discourage her, but I knew it would take her another eight years, at least, to finish her undergraduate work as well as law school. I didn't know if she had the necessary persistence. What I didn't realize at the time was that she had an enormous need for achievement, and nothing would stop her. Gretchen is now a very successful attorney in Miami.

Characteristics of People with a Strong Need to Achieve

Persons high in need for achievement usually are hardworking and energetic, determined and productive. They relish being known as people who get things done with precision, skill, and accuracy. Nearly everything they do is on purpose. They're clear in their goals and move toward them in a straight, purposeful direction—no sidetracking, no messing around with doubts, no wheel-spinning. If they want to become head of the department, or head of the company, nothing is going to move them off the straight track upward. They don't put off till tomorrow what can be done today. Persistence is their trademark. They're well organized, clear in their goals, and know what must be done to attain success. Confidence in their ability makes them unafraid to try new things. They don't mind change; they even enjoy it. They take on responsibility easily, even when it takes them over their heads, and even when the fault lies elsewhere. They feel responsible for everyone they work with. They accept constructive criticism very well. Most of the time, they use the criticism to learn how to avoid future mistakes and to help insure their success. Although they may take it personally, they blame themselves rather than the person who offered the criticism.

High-need achievers have a tendency, sometimes, to move too fast and to try to do too many things at one time. They're perfectionists to the limit. They expect 110 percent from themselves and from others, and are often disappointed when they don't give it or get it. They expect to have all the right answers, to say all the right things. They hate to ask for help, because they see this as a weakness in themselves. For that reason, high-need achievers find it very difficult to delegate work to others. People very high in the need for achievement may negatively prejudge people who don't meet their standards, either in terms of work accomplishment, commitment to the job or organization, or different motivation needs. They make very poor team players, unless members of their team are at least as capable professionally as they are. They have been known to exaggerate, especially in terms of their expectations. In budgeting for next year's sales estimates, they tend to estimate sales at a highly optimistic rather than realistic level.

For example, Burt, an advertising sales manager for a radio station, almost lost his job after two successive years of moderate increases in revenue. "The general manager was happy with the increases," Burt related, "but furious at me because I said we'd get a 30 percent increase and only came up by 10 percent. I can understand why he was unhappy, because my overestimates made him look bad to the station owner. I had depended on my salespersons' estimates, but soon learned to take their figures and cut them way down."

Good communication is not one of the assets of persons with a high need for achievement. They tend to be poor listeners (they know the answer before you ask the question), are sometimes garrulous, and are so busy rationalizing their feelings that they tend to block out their emotions. Because they hold in their emotions, high-need-for-achievement people may let hurts and rejections build up until they're ready to burst. It's difficult for them to tell you how they *feel*, although they're always ready to tell you their *beliefs*.

Other Research

John Holland did some interesting research from the mid-1950s to the mid 1960s connecting personality traits with occupations.[4] Although Holland used different terminology and a different theory, his work confirms the idea of matching people to jobs. Three of his personality types are nearly identical to persons with a high need for achievement.

A *realistic personality*, according to Holland, often displays aggressive behavior and prefers activities requiring skill, strength and coordination. This type values rewards such as money and possessions and tends to see the world in simple, tangible, and traditional terms. Sample occupations good for a realistic personality are mechanical engineer, plumber, auto mechanic, veterinarian, and forklift operator.

An *investigative personality* fosters cognitive behavior and prefers thinking, organizing, and understanding activities. They're rewarded not by money but by public acceptance of their scientific accomplishment. They see the world in complex, abstract, independent, and original ways. Sample occupations ideal for an investigative personality include physicist, weather observer, and laboratory assistant.

Finally, Holland describes the *artistic personality*, which encourages self-expressive behavior, and prefers artistic, self-fulfilling, and individualistic activities. Their reward is in the display of their artistic talent. They tend to see the world in complex, independent, unconventional, and flexible ways. Sample occupations for the artistic personality are copy or book editor, decorator, garment designer, and fashion artist.

Other researchers have found that high-need-for-achievement people *expect success*, and when they get it they tend to attribute that success to internal factors, such as ability and effort. When they fail, they attribute the failure to external factors, such as luck. Low-need achievers, on the other hand, say their success is due to luck or ease of the task, while failure is due to low ability and effort.

Logical and Scientific Thinking

Some of our best scientists and engineers are people high in need for achievement. They do extremely well in applying principles of logical or scientific thinking to a wide range of intellectual and practical problems. They're able to deal with nonverbal symbolism—such as formulas, scientific equations, graphs, and musical notes—in its most difficult forms. They can handle a wide variety of abstract and concrete variables, and understand even the most ambiguous and obscure concepts. They're good at applying logic and scientific thinking to define problems, collect data, establish facts, and draw valid conclusions. Also, they're great at interpreting an extensive variety of technical instructions in books and manuals, both in mathematical and diagrammatic forms.

This ability is not limited to theoretical situations. High-need achievers can be very practical in the way they apply their logical and scientific thinking. They're excellent at solving practical problems, dealing with a wide variety of concrete variables in situations where only limited standardization exists. And, regardless of format—written, oral, diagrammatic, or schedule—they're able to interpret and carry out instructions quite easily.

Managers Who Have a High Need for Achievement

Managers who have a high need for achievement concentrate their efforts on personal accomplishment and improvement. They tend to be highly independent individuals who want to assume responsibility and credit for task accomplishment and who want short-term concrete feedback on their performance so they know how well they're doing. These characteristics often are closely associated with *entrepreneurial* success. These same characteristics can be detrimental where the individual has to manage others, however. In complex organizations, managers obviously can't perform all the tasks necessary for success; teamwork is necessary. Also, feedback on the group's effort and performance is often vague and delayed. For that reason, the managerial environment is not totally suitable for stimulating the achievement motivation in managers.

Keep in mind that most high-need-for-achievement people are more interested in the task than they are in relationships with people. For that reason, they're likely to be poor in people skills, to be authoritarian in management style, and to make poor managers. They're usually great in entrepreneurial jobs. They're innovative, and especially good in problem-solving situations.

An MBA student, Dick, was in the accelerated program at the University of Colorado at Denver. He had worked for a major aerospace manufacturer in the Denver area for about fifteen years and held a master's degree in electrical engineering. He had been promoted into management jobs several times. Each time, his department increased productivity, but he left a trail of broken spirits among his employees. Fortunately for him and for his subordinates, he was on a fast track and was moved out of each position within a year or two. He had a reputation for brilliance but an equal reputation for being an abrasive, hostile, inflexible manager. When we first met in class, Dick had been fired from his aerospace job despite his knack for getting things done. I suggested to Dick that he consider starting his own business, where he could concentrate his efforts on creating new products rather than managing people.

Sex Differences in Need for Achievement

Although early researchers found women to have a lower need for achievement than men—possibly because the need to compete was considered a "masculine" attribute—most studies now show that women generally have the same need for achievement that men do. But certain women tend to be lower in need for achievement, while others are higher.

Homemakers see themselves as rather conforming, conventional, dependent, and not at all competitive. Their concerns about academic or family role achievement are not necessarily translated to personal career ambitions. Women in this group avoid risks and conflict and are likely to be more fearful and anxious—traits that reduce a person's need for achievement.

Older women who have worked for many years may not have very high work-oriented achievement needs. They were brought up to believe that personal growth and achievement come from being competent at home, not at work. Parents and teachers of women who are now between the ages of forty and sixty were likely to have reinforced the notion that satisfaction in a woman's life comes from the traditional family role. While the majority of women in this age group may be low in need for achievement, a growing contingent now find that self-fulfillment comes from a creative, challenging job. Fulfillment of their need for achievement is especially crucial.

Married female professionals are more assertive and competitive than women who choose to stay at home. Although they're usually dependent in their personal lives, they're quite independent at work, are very active, and have a low rating on conventionality. A challenging job is very important to them. Their need for achievement will be about the same as most males'.

According to Jane, a married, forty-one-year-old bank teller, "For the first thirteen years of my marriage, my family was all I needed. But then I found something was missing. I didn't feel fulfilled. When I started working, I got good vibes from my job. It made me feel important, like I had something going for me."

Single professional females, workers under thirty, and women managers regardless of marital status are very strong in the need for achievement—much higher, in fact, than male workers or managers. They want to be financially independent of men. They tend to be more secure, have less sex-role conflict, and are convinced they're just as capable of handling their jobs as men. They're looking for a challenge at work and for advancement opportunities. They're very competitive, task-oriented, rational in their thinking, and exert strong personal effort to accomplish their goals. They're not dependent at work or in their personal lives. Today, increases in nontraditional values among women make it more socially acceptable both to compete and to succeed.

Jobs That Fulfill the Need for Achievement

You took the motivation need test. You know that you have a dominant need for achievement. Now you also know what that means in terms of your personality traits and characteristics. You also know how you differ from your colleagues of the opposite sex, and what impact a high need for achievement has on your chances of being a good manager. The rest of this chapter will show you how to be happy at work.

As I pointed out in the preface, this book may change your life. The Appendix list of high-need-for-achievement jobs and occupations (see page 121) offers an opportunity you don't want to miss. The list is especially valuable for several categories of people.

Persons Who Are Unhappy at Work but Not Sure Why

Check the list of jobs that fulfill the need for achievement. Is your job included in that list? If you have a high need for achievement and you're unhappy with your present job, the chances are your job or occupation is *not* on the list.

That means you are now in a job that is not designed to fulfill your needs. But since there are many other jobs that you would find satisfying, you don't have to accept being miserable at work.

We've listed one hundred of the most popular jobs that satisfy the need for achievement in the appendix. Think about which of those jobs you already are qualified to do. Those probably should be your first choice. There are others, however, that may take a little extra training but won't require more than a few months of reschooling. These probably should be your second choice.

Have you ever considered making a major career change? If so, this may be the right time to do it. Check the list carefully. If it contains a job or career that you've always thought you'd enjoy, your instincts were absolutely correct.

Persons Trying to Decide on a Long-term Career Path

Whether you're happy or unhappy at work in your present job, it's important to know how well you will match the *next* job on your promotion ladder. For those with a very high need for achievement, consider the alternatives very carefully before you accept a promotion to management.

Persons in Fields Where Job Opportunities Are Narrowing Because of Mergers Competition New Products

Before you decide to make a move to another field, make sure it contains jobs that will fulfill your needs. Don't pick a field just because jobs are available. If you choose a job you're not suited for motivationally, you'll only end up making a second move in two to five years.

Students Who Must Decide on a College Major

By matching your motivation profile with the appropriate job, you can choose the career that will make you happy, rather than the career that might get you a quick job out of college but long-term discontent. For those with a dominant need for achievement, stay away from majors such as education, nursing, management, religion, journalism, or criminal justice. There are many other majors more suitable. Just check the list.

Women Who Want to Return to the Work Force

It's important to remember that the skills you learned while running your household and managing your family may easily be applied to any number of "just-right" jobs on this list. You probably already are qualified for some. But with the maturity and judgment you've acquired from your previous duties, you may find that going back to school is easier and more practical than you ever dreamed. Some of the most successful career people are former homemakers.

How Jim Ferguson Became Happy at Work

Jim Ferguson, you'll recall, a self-employed tax accountant, was very unhappy at work once his company expanded and he had to spend most of his time managing others. He wasn't sure why it was happening, but his business was going down the drain because he was losing both clients and some of his key professional and staff personnel. He telephoned me for help. After studying his problem and interviewing his employees. I guessed the problem involved a mismatch between his motivation needs and his relatively new managerial responsibilities. I asked him to fill out the "Manifest Needs Questionnaire." Results showed that Jim had a very high need for achievement—perfect for the tax accountant job he used to do all the time but no longer had much time for. Even though he still considered himself a tax accountant by profession, his real job now was that of a manager. That job fulfills the need for power, and is a poor choice for someone like Jim who has a high need for achievement.

One possible answer to Jim's problem was to reduce the size of his practice to the point where he again could handle it by himself. That way, he would no longer have to supervise anyone except for a secretary or receptionist. If Jim were much older and wasn't locked in to his present life-style, that might have been a good solution.

But it wasn't practical for Jim to give up his business. He needed the income a large practice offered in order to send his two teenage sons to college and to keep up his beautiful home in suburban Denver. Also, his wife, Sally, was not happy in her job either, and they were faced with the possibility that she might have to give up working.

The Solution

I suggested to Jim that he take in a partner. He needed to find another accountant with an understanding of tax work, but with a high need for power—a partner who enjoyed having impact and influence over others. That way, the partner's job would be to manage all the other accountants, leaving Jim time to do what he did best and most enjoyed. Jim and I worked together to find a talented accountant with a dominant need for power, and he sold him a half-interest in the practice. Although the new partner was young and lacked some of Jim's expertise in accounting, his people skills were excellent. It didn't take long for the staff to respond to him, and within a year of the partnership, the practice started to expand once more. This time, however, they were easily able to handle the extra business. Both Jim and the partner enjoy their work and their relationship.

How to Be Happier at Work Without Changing Jobs

Many people don't want to change jobs even though they're unhappy at work. That's understandable. Perhaps it's too difficult to find a new job. Many sections of the country are in the middle of an economic slowdown. New jobs may be tough to find. Perhaps you need the steady income and can't afford the few weeks or months it may take to relocate. Some jobs pay extremely high salaries, and even though they may not be fulfilling your motivation needs, the money is very important to you or to your family. Other people may not want to risk trying a new job or career.

Whatever your reason may be for not changing to a job that is a good fit for your motivation need profile, there are still many things you can do to become a happier, more fulfilled person.

Things You Can Do at Work to Help Fulfill Your Need for Achievement

1. Accept assignments that involve a *moderate* risk. If the likelihood of success is too low or too high, you won't be satisfied.
2. Volunteer to participate in departmental planning.
3. Join task forces set up to solve department or company problems.
4. Ask your manager for an appointment at least once a month to discuss the quality and progress of your work.
5. Know your career goals. Check with your friends to make sure they're reasonable and attainable.
6. Decide on the job you want next. Make sure you learn all the skills necessary and then tell your boss that you are qualified for that job and want it.
7. Check with customers to find out if they're satisfied. Help them solve their problems with your company.
8. Figure out how to correct your own errors or quality problems before they reach the inspector or customer.
9. Try to find a new or better way to do each part of your present job.

10. Find a mentor at work to help you get ahead. Don't be afraid to ask for help and advice. It is not a sign of weakness, but a smart move in your path upward.

11. Make sure that time is not your greatest enemy. If you have overcommitted your time, step back a little. Reassess your expectations. Prioritize what needs to be done. Be flexible.

12. Allow yourself to make an honest mistake. No one is perfect, including you. You'll be much more relaxed once you're able to accept 90 percent perfection.

13. Set your own standards if you believe the company's standards for your job are too low.

14. Work off tension if you're worried or aggravated. Both disappear when work begins.

15. Test your capabilities. Stretch your talents. Try harder to do tasks you've never done before.

16. Pat yourself on the back when you do something well. If your boss doesn't know enough to recognize good work, you do.

17. Instead of worrying about not being good enough for the next job, concentrate on being the very best in the business at your present job.

18. Plan ahead. Make a list of things you need to do. Take it one step at a time. As you accomplish a task, cross it off the list. Getting even a small job out of the way will give you a feeling of accomplishment.

19. Don't give up if you fail, even though it hurts. Give yourself credit for having tried, and look for other areas of opportunity.

20. Show the following suggestions to your manager. Each time the boss gets one of them done, your

motivation will increase and you will become a better, more productive worker. Tell your boss that this is an excellent way to increase productivity and profits for the company.

Things Your Manager Can Do at Work to Help Fulfill Your Need for Achievement

1. Encourage you to get involved in planning.
2. Give you freedom to make decisions about your own hours and work methods.
3. Give you creative work to perform.
4. Make sure you see the final results of your work.
5. Show you how your job fits into the "total picture."
6. Give you frequent feedback. The feedback should be constructive, but may be positive or negative. You need to find out what to do to improve.
7. Place you in a job where you can assume personal responsibility for your actions.
8. Grant you additional authority in your activity. In other words, allow you more job freedom.
9. Introduce you to new and more difficult tasks not previously handled.
10. Assign you specific or specialized task, enabling you to become an "expert."
11. Remove some controls over your work, while retaining the manager's accountability.
12. Increase your accountability for your own work.
13. Make periodic reports, such as budget comparisons, available to you.
14. Rotate your job duties with that of another employee so that both of you may use a greater variety of skills.
15. Send you to training sessions to increase your skills and abilities.

Things You Can Do at Home to Fulfill Your Need for Achievement

1. Expand your areas of interest and involvement. Start doing what you've always dreamed of doing. It makes no difference if it involves playing a musical instrument or planting and maintaining a beautiful flower or vegetable garden in the backyard. Try it. If you don't like it, find something else to do.

2. Go back to school part-time. Every community offers evening classes in subjects that will intrigue and challenge you. Unless you choose to, you don't have to take them for credit or obligate yourself to do homework.

3. Daydream. It's okay to do. Fantasizing success makes you feel good. Visualize yourself being successful. Research shows that those who believe they can succeed are most likely to succeed.

4. Set up a workshop to make wood or metal accessories.

5. Work out at a health club. Decide what you want to accomplish and stick with it until you do.

6. Take up any competitive athletic activity such as golf, tennis, swimming, softball, or running. Set your own goals and objectives and try to meet or exceed them.

7. Write a short story or a book.

8. Start a hobby. How about photography, wood- or metal-working, stamp or coin collecting?

9. Take up needlepoint, crewel, knitting, or crocheting. These help fulfill your creative and achievement needs.

10. Try your hand at crossword or jigsaw puzzles. They're challenging and fun.

11. Cherish your achievement. You have a tendency to be overambitious and to move too fast to enjoy the fruits of your accomplishments. At night, when you have time to relax, think about what you accomplished that day. Remember your most recent success or achievement. Enjoy the good feeling it brings.

NOTES

1. David C. McClelland, John W. Atkinson, Russell A. Clark, and Edgar L. Lowell, *The Achievement Motive* (New York: Appleton-Century-Crofts, 1953), p. 111.
2. McClelland, *The Achieving Society* (New York: The Free Press, 1961), p. 437.
3. Atkinsons, ed., *Motives in Fantasy, Actions, and Society* (Princeton, NJ: Van Nostrand, 1958).
4. John L. Holland, "A Theory of Occupational Choice," *Journal of Counseling Psychology*, vol. 6 (1959), pp. 34–45; Holland, "A Psychological Classification Scheme for Vocations and Major Fields," *Journal of Counseling Psychology*, vol. 13 (1966), pp. 278–288; Holland, D. R. Whitney, N. S. Cole, and J. M. Richards, Jr., "An Empirical Occupational Classification Derived from a Theory of Personality and Intended for Practice and Research," ACT Research Report No. 29 (Iowa City, IA: The American College Testing Program, 1969).

7 Affiliation: The Joy of Working With Friends

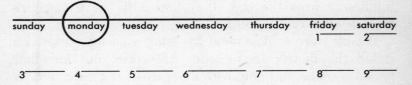

sunday	monday	tuesday	wednesday	thursday	friday	saturday
					1	2
3	4	5	6	7	8	9

If need for achievement is the drive that energized America's entrepreneurial spirit, need for affiliation is the one that nurtured it, that allowed it to work so well in thousands of factories throughout the U.S. When Henry Ford designed his first assembly line, his innovativeness and high need for achievement brought him success and wealth. The assembly line also brought a new group of employees the opportunity to fulfill their need for affiliation. Before that, only skilled craftsmen and auto mechanics built automobiles. They did so by hand, depending on a work ethic that respected high-quality work, a diversity of skills, and a desire to create or produce something better than had been done before. Like Ford, these workers were high in the need for achievement. But the assembly line and automation created a series of routine, boring jobs that changed the needs that were fulfilled for America's work force from high levels of need for achievement to high levels of need for affiliation.

Because assembly-line jobs are routine and boring, they offer little satisfaction. Instead, these jobs offer employees an opportunity to work alongside others and to develop camaraderie. When need-for-achievement workers aren't fulfilled by the task itself, they will leave the job. Other workers—those with need for affiliation—don't look for fulfillment from the task; they find it in the friendships they develop on the job.

We measure achievement by using a positive approach called the motive to succeed. Affiliation, on the other hand, is concerned only with a negative. It's measured by the fear of rejection rather than the pleasure of being accepted. The need for security is another integral part of the need for affiliation.

"My brother Morris is very competitive," thirty-eight-year-old Jerry told the motivation workshop I conducted last year. "And I think that's just terrific for him. But I don't understand how he can put up with the rejection all the time. He's a telemarketing salesman and probably the best his company has. But he tells me he's lucky if he can make a sale to three out of each hundred phone calls. He laughed at me when I asked him how he could stand the other ninety-seven people hanging up on him or rejecting him. I'd be devastated," Jerry confessed to the group. "Thank God I don't have to face that doing my kind of work." Jerry is a proofreader for the local newspaper. "It may not be the most exciting job in the world," he said, "but it's pretty good knowing my buddies look forward to our getting together every day too."

From birth, babies appear to need some form of social connection. Otherwise, infants' normal physical and personality development is slowed. Parents of children high in need for affiliation probably emphasized close family ties and the dependency during the children's early years, increasing anxiety levels as well as affiliation motivation.

Affiliation also appears to be related to conformity, although the exact nature of that relationship isn't very clear. Some writers contend that persons who fear rejection learn that it's safer to submit and conform because there's little chance of social disapproval and threat to self-esteem. They feel much more secure when they conform to the wishes of others and receive their approval. So they tend to agree with the judgment of groups and seldom exercise much independent thought. Other writers favor the theory of rejection anxiety and subsequent conformity, but see positive rather than negative outcomes. They point to people who have adjusted to those fears by modifying their behavior to include such attributes as love, friendship, warm, personal social ties, empathy and understanding, and the need to help others when asked.

Characteristics of People With a Strong Need for Affiliation

Regardless of what causes the motivation drive, the need for affiliation simply is the need for close, interpersonal relationships and friendships with other people.

Workers high in this need want approval, belonging, and friendship. They feel a strong need to be accepted and to feel part of the group. They want to be reassured; they want to know they are valued and loved. They're often open and responsive. They want friends. They're not as concerned with getting ahead as high-need achievers, but enjoy jobs that offer many interactions with people. They have a sincere interest in the feelings of others.

At work they tend to avoid conflict and criticism and take jobs with a lot of interpersonal contact. They have better attendance records than those with low affiliation need.[1] They also perform somewhat better in situations where personal support and approval are tied to performance.[2] To the extent that supervisors can create a cooperative, supportive work environment where positive feedback is tied to task performance, affiliation-need employees often are more productive. They enjoy cooperating with others more than working by themselves and are much more effective when placed in groups with a cooperative spirit than in competitive groups. They exhibit empathy and understanding and express by their actions the need to help others and solve their problems.

For example, George, a twenty-seven-year-old factory supervisor for an aerospace manufacturer in Denver, works mostly on project teams, each of which handles a particular missile or plane. George's group of twelve people (two each from six departments) had been working together for more than two years when George told the rest of his management class about how project teams work in his industry. "We're like the Denver Broncos football team," he explained. "Of course, we have one extra player, which the Broncos could use sometimes, but every one of us has our own specialized job to do. We can't score unless we all pull together. We all respect each other, and when we have a problem the team works it out."

Studies have uncovered several problems with high-affiliation-need workers. One researcher warns that they may be so concerned with fostering warm, interpersonal relationships that job performance falls off.[3] Another reports that they make more nonbusiness local phone calls on the job, write more letters to friends, and spend more time visiting with people they enjoy than those low in affiliation need.[4] They have a tendency to conform to the wishes and norms of others when pressured by friends. Because they're afraid to be deviates in a cohesive group, they tend to accommodate themselves to the others in order to avoid undermining the group's camaraderie or appearing to be "nervous nellies." This often results in "group-think" tendencies, which focus so strongly on maintaining congeniality and a positive group atmosphere that the group fails to evaluate information critically. Because high-affiliation-need people like to made decisions in groups, they tend to take greater risks than when making decisions alone, increasing the likelihood of failure when risk-taking isn't considered carefully. If given a choice, high-affiliation-need people choose to work on committees with people they like rather than with experts. For that reason, committees filled with affiliation-need members may not be as effective as they should be.

In their personal lives, they're in their element when they're with a group of people who enjoy life. They become very attached to friends, and when they fall in love they give in utterly to the happiness that love brings. Generally, they don't enjoy being alone for long periods of time, and readily accept social invitations rather than staying home. If the invitation is to a party or some type of large social gathering, they look forward to the evening eagerly. They enjoy playing around, especially with people who don't take life too seriously. But they don't need formal parties to enjoy themselves and to express cordiality and good will to others. One of the best ways they can think of to spend an afternoon or evening is to hang around with a group of congenial people to talk about anything that comes up. Even in new groups they make friends quickly, because they feel at ease in a few minutes, and tend to have a good word for most people. They're always on the lookout for more friends, no matter how many they already have. Other people enjoy being with them, because high-need-for-affiliation individuals make a special effort to promote good feelings.

When I did some consulting for one of the local hospitals, I interviewed the head of the pathology department, a forty-seven-year-old woman named Mollie. I asked Mollie to tell me about the one thing that pleased her most about her staff and about the doctor who headed the lab. She related how she felt when she first got the job after moving to Denver from a similar position in Milwaukee. "I couldn't believe my eyes when I first got here," she said. "Doctor Jim knew every one of his pathology workers like he knew his own family. It seemed like they'd talk or crack jokes half the day. Every time one of the doctors or nurses from another department came in for something, Doctor Jim would take the time to say hello and find out how they were doing. I was used to a much more business-like department, where everybody thinks of themself as a scientist and keeps their eyes glued to the microscope. I was uncomfortable about it in the beginning, but I felt myself being drawn up into this cocoon of friendship and good will. I have lots of friends outside of work, but there's no such thing as too many. I don't know how the work gets done sometimes, but our record speaks for itself."

Researchers have consistently linked high need for affiliation with good health. One researcher found that high-affiliation-need male college graduates in their middle thirties had lower-than-average blood pressure, and that similar but older males in their mid-fifties had a less severe record of illnesses.[5] Another study tested male prisoners and found that their immune defense system was in better order than prisoners high in other needs, particularly in fighting viral infections.[6] And dental students high in affiliation need were better able to ward off colds.[7]

Psychologist David McClelland tells about some fasci-nat-ing research he and one of his students did that looked at the relation between motivation need scores and health. They gave a motivation test to a group of people one day and took saliva samples to check on concentrations of immunoglobulin A (S-IgA), "the body's first line of defense against viral infections, particularly those of the upper respiratory tract.[8] A few days later, the same subjects came to the laboratory again in small groups to view films designed to arouse different motivational states. One film was designed to arouse power scores and showed Hitler's early successes in World War II. The other film was a documentary about Mother Teresa, the nun who has devoted her life to helping the poor, the sick, and the dying. That film successfully increased levels of need for affiliation. In contrast to the film about Hitler, the Mother Teresa film produced a significant increase in S-IgA concentrations immediately, suggesting, according to McClelland, that "Mother Teresa's capacity for loving had evoked a similar response in the viewers, which had a beneficial effect on their body's defense against disease." This study and several others showed a direct link between good health and affiliative motives—the capacity to love and be loved.

Need for Affiliation and Managerial Behavior

For obvious reasons, people who try to avoid conflict and criticism make poor managers. Yet this avoidance is a major characteristic of men and women who are high in need for affiliation. It's not surprising, then, that research shows that individuals high in this motive rarely succeed as managers of people. At AT&T, young men high in affiliation need were reported not to get promoted as often to higher levels of management, and firms headed by need-for-affiliation chief executive officers were less successful than those headed by high-need-for-power or need-for-achievement executives.[9] Most management jobs need people who are competitive, who try to influence others, and who aren't afraid to make tough, unpopular decisions that may hurt other people's feelings. Because high-need-for-affiliation people hate conflict, they avoid it.

Let me give an example. Billy was brilliant. If you asked him to redesign a piece of equipment to increase productivity he could come up with an answer in a couple of days. He started with his electronics firm at twenty-one, right out of college. By twenty-three he was made supervisor, and by twenty-six he was promoted to department head. By twenty-eight Billy was demoted. Not because he wasn't still brilliant, or hardworking. He was demoted because within two years his department was loaded with deadwood, people who weren't producing and should have been replaced. Billy couldn't bring himself to tell his employees that they were doing unsatisfactory work. He was afraid he'd be unpopular, and even more afraid the employee would make a scene. Instead, he just kept everyone on the payroll, good or bad. It cost him his managerial job.

High-affiliation-need managers enjoy working with people they like rather than with experts they don't like, so their departments often aren't as productive as others, or provide less efficient customer service. Managers like Billy don't enjoy or need power, so they seek it much less than other managers. When they are promoted into powerful positions, they diminish their power by not using it. As a result, affiliative managers are unable to get the resources they need for their departments and are unable to get promotions and raises for their worthy employees.

The management information systems department of a Miami transportation company was run by Marvin, a very affable and capable professional whose slow rise up the ranks was due to his technical skills and friendly personality. I met Marvin a few years ago when the executive vice-president of the company called me to find out why the MIS department had by far the highest turnover rate of any department in the company.

"It's a mystery to us," the executive V.P. told me, "because the head of the department—Marvin—is very well liked by everyone. His department, though, seems to get bogged down in unfinished projects, and he's already lost six of his best people, who moved on to other companies. What's wrong?" he asked.

After talking to Marvin and several of his colleagues, I soon realized that he was viewed by his peers as a weakling who couldn't push his people to get things moving. Three of the six employees left when they received barely minimum raises, and two left because of a long-standing work overload when the same executive V.P. refused to let Marvin hire another programmer to get out the work. Nice-guy Marvin turned out to be a powerless, overly affiliative manager who couldn't get necessary resources for his workers. So they quit.

Another major managerial function is helping others to achieve. Need-for-power managers love influencing others, so they'll try to help workers whether the workers ask for help or not. Need-for-affiliation managers, though, don't want to "interfere" with other people's lives, so they won't offer any help unless asked. Achieving is a fundamental goal of every organization, a fundamental hope for nearly every individual. Unless managers help employees achieve, they're not doing their job properly.

Some contend that high-affiliation-need managers avoid helping or influencing others because they're afraid of being rejected, afraid of being disliked. They're also afraid of criticizing their employees because they believe everyone hates criticism, as they do. They're wrong, though. Some workers thrive on criticism, particularly those high in need for achievement.

For instance, Delores is a thirty-five-year-old university researcher who used to work in a similar job for a scientific government agency. "I was in shock," she told me, "when

I came in to work one morning—after working there for two years—and my boss, Sylvia, called me into her office and told me that she was forced to let me go because I wasn't producing up to the agency's quota standards. 'What quota standards?' I asked her? 'I never knew we had a quota for how much we had to turn out. You always told me I was doing wonderful work here and that my quality was better than anyone else's! If I had known I needed to research more quantity, you should have told me so I could've changed what I was doing.' Can you imagine, my boss actually had tears in her eyes when she turned to me and said she never said anything before because she didn't want to hurt my feelings, but that I should've known since quotas were posted up on the bulletin board. I could've screamed," Delores said, still trembling with anger and frustration about a firing that took place nearly a year ago. "That weak jerk," she said, "cost me my job and my self-respect by not having enough guts to set me straight right away when I could've done something about it."

It's a sad fact that the more managers high in affiliation need avoid conflict and competition, and the more they seek approval, the *less* popular they become.[10] Employees feel uncomfortable with bosses who spend so much time seeking assurances from others. Other reasons that high-need-for-affiliation managers make poor bosses is that they tend to be anxious about their relations with others, hate being in the spotlight, and particularly dislike others who disagree with them. Since managers constantly face all those situations, their need for affiliation drags them down.

Sex Differences in Need for Affiliation

Early research evidence (now mostly debunked) pointed to males being motivated by need for achievement and females by need for affiliation. Some researchers believed that when women did achieve, it was out of a need for affiliation or acceptance. There was—and still is—some acceptance of the theory that when both sexes are very young, they strive for acceptance from others. As they get older, however, boys internalize their approval drives by looking for self-acceptance; girls generally hold on to their external need to be accepted and approved by parents and friends. In the early 1960s most researchers believed that success was not a goal in itself for women, but only a means of attaining social approval. In the 1970s it was generally accepted that women had a higher need for affiliation than men, and that the achievement behavior women did show was fueled by their need to please. If the two needs (achievement and affiliation) were in conflict, women would be more apt than men to reduce their need for achievement behavior and thereby reduce the anxiety caused by the conflict.

Social values have changed—to a great degree because of the women's movement. Accompanying that change in values is a dramatic change in sex differences in need for affiliation. More than ever before, women are less concerned with and less fearful of rejection by others. They have more confidence in themselves and show increasing concern for self-approval rather than external approval. Also, more women than ever work, often in formerly male-dominated occupations.

Motivation theorists in the 1980s now believe that women in general still have a higher need for affiliation than men in general, but the differences are very slight when we look only at working women and men, and they disappear completely at the managerial and professional levels.[11]

Jobs that Fulfill the Need for Affiliation

Okay, let's assume you have a high need for affiliation. You already know that it may present a lot of problems if you're a manager or aspire to be one. If you read the chapter on need for achievement, then you also know there are at least one hundred jobs that fulfill the need for achievement but won't help fulfill your needs. I've told the story of Jim and Sally Ferguson: Sally was a computer programmer who loved the money she made but hated her job. It fulfilled the need for achievement, but Sally's test scores—like yours—showed that she had a high need for affiliation, *not* achievement.

How Sally Fulfilled Her Need for Affiliation

I was able to help Sally Ferguson, but in a way different from the way I helped her husband, Jim. Jim brought in a partner who was perfectly suited to manage his accounting and office personnel, leaving Jim to concentrate on what fulfilled his needs—his work as a tax accountant. Sally, however, worked for someone else. She could have tried to make the best of a bad situation by finding ways to satisfy her affiliation needs on the job, but computer programmers work mostly alone, making it especially difficult to develop friendships and warm, personal relationships on the job. If you're the major support of a family or have to depend on your own earnings to survive, it may be difficult to leave a job, especially one you're good at technically, in search of a happier, more fulfilling job. But it made much more sense for Sally Ferguson to leave her job as a computer programmer. Her husband, Jim, made a fine living as an accountant, and while they were happy having her computer programmer income, they could afford to lose that income while Sally retrained herself for a more appropriate occupation.

I showed Sally the same list of one hundred jobs that appears in the Appendix. Every one of those jobs predominantly fulfills the need for affiliation—Sally's dominant need and that of millions of American men and women.

She selected five jobs that looked especially interesting, and we spent the afternoon discussing the pros and cons of each.

The five jobs that appealed to Sally at first glance were: day care center worker, exerciser, hostess, masseuse (massage therapist), and nurse. The day care center job was eliminated because Sally felt she had done that type of work raising her own children and really wanted a change of pace. Being a hostess in a restaurant was impractical because it involved being away more at night than she was willing to be. She liked the idea of rehabilitating people through massage therapy, but eventually that was eliminated as well because a check through the yellow pages and newspaper ads showed that her community was filled with dozens of masseuses looking for clients.

That left two very different jobs with appeal to Sally. The first was as an exerciser. Sally was very fit and trim and attended aerobics classes three times a week. She loved the way exercise helped her to reduce stress and keep slim. Also, she met lots of new people at aerobics class and remembered fondly the friends she'd made. "Maybe I could open up my own aerobics studio," she speculated. Her second good possibility was nursing. Her father had been a doctor but hadn't spent much time with his family when she grew up. She knew she could never be happy doing that, but had always shared her father's love of medicine. There was a shortage of registered nurses, the profession paid very well, and helping others was a powerful attraction to Sally.

Sally finally decided on aerobics, although it was a tough decision. Nursing would require several years of training, while she already had the necessary aerobics skills. She was good at math, had a fine understanding of business, and had a husband who solemnly promised to do her accounting and bookkeeping for no charge. Within six months Sally left her old job, opened her own studio, and was on her way to a happy career that kept her close to people yet allowed ample time for her family.

How to Be Happier at Work Without Changing Jobs

It may not make much sense right now to change jobs. It's one thing to be unhappy at work, but even worse not to have a job. Unless, of course, there is a shortage of workers in a particular field, and you have confidence that it won't take too long to get a new position. Some people are so unhappy at work they just can't stay in their present job anymore. That's understandable, and, despite the risk, they ought to make the change as soon as possible. For others, it may not be practical to change to a job that's a better fit for their motivation profile. If you're one of those, there still are many things you can do to become a happier, more fulfilled person.

Things You Can Do at Work to Help Fulfill Your Need for Affiliation

1. Volunteer to work on committees, but never as leader of the group.
2. Ask to have your desk moved to be nearer to fellow workers.
3. Ask to be transferred to any task that requires you to work as a team member.
4. Take responsibility for contacts with customers or the public.
5. Convince your boss you'd be a great candidate for the job when a liaison is needed between departments.

6. Continue to be open and responsive to others at work. The chances are good that others doing work similar to yours also appreciate those qualities.
7. Keep your antennae alert to the needs of coworkers.
8. Join the union, social activities club, or any charitable group at work that helps people in the community.
9. Join your colleagues after work in some relaxing way, by having a drink or a snack before going home.
10. Participate in company athletic teams, even though you may not be a star.
11. Practice saying no until it becomes easier and easier.
12. Remember that making no decision is worse than making a wrong decision.
13. Volunteer to coordinate the work of others, such as specialists, or the work of departments.
14. Save time during the work day to interact with coworkers on non-work activities.
15. Concentrate on long-term worker relationships.
16. Get involved in group projects.
17. Carpool to work.
18. Go out to lunch with coworkers. Don't eat at your desk.
19. Join a professional group.

Things Your Manager Can Do at Work to Help Fulfill Your Need for Affiliation

1. Give you an opportunity for interaction with others.
2. Help you develop compatible work groups.
3. Instill a feeling of team spirit at work.
4. Be friendly and personable to you.
5. When you do something well, praise, approve, and encourage you to continue.
6. Make you feel secure about your job and work relationships.
7. Reassure you that you are liked and valued.

8. Allow you and your friends to talk together during the day as long as your work gets done.
9. Never erect partitions between you and your coworkers.
10. Keep your work environment friendly and pleasant.
11. Show you understanding and empathy.
12. Understand that you sometimes may be indecisive in decision-making. Be patient with you as you are helped to make those decisions.
13. Reward your commitment to the department or the company with praise and acceptance.
14. Let you help organize the company picnic.
15. Place you in a job that requires integrating the goals of various workers or departments with the organization's goals.
16. Take you out for lunch. Tell you what a good job you're doing, and how much you've contributed to the organization.

Things You Can Do at Home to Fulfill Your Need for Affiliation

1. If you are not married, be sure never to live alone. Take in a roommate.
2. Go to that interesting party you heard about. If your spouse doesn't want to go, go alone. It's okay.
3. Every time you pass a greeting card store, buy some cards that express the feelings you may be too shy to express yourself. Address an envelope, put on a stamp, and mail one right now! It'll make you feel wonderful.
4. Put aside thirty minutes each day after work to spend "alone" time with your spouse or significant other. If you have children, tell them that they must not disturb you, during that time. Give them thirty minutes of "alone" time, also.

5. Attend church or synagogue if you are religious.
6. Go out of your way to be with your friends.
7. Feel free in expressing cordiality and good will to others.
8. Telephone a friend as soon as your household chores are out of the way.
9. Stay away from acquaintances who don't enjoy life.
10. Make up a reminder calendar with the birthdays and anniversaries of all your friends. Buy all the greeting cards at the beginning of each month and mail them a few days before the occasion. Soon, your friends will be sending you cards, too.
11. Open yourself to the love of humanity in general. Otherwise, you cannot be in love with life.
12. Say hello to one person in every shopping aisle when you shop next in the supermarket.
13. Confide your innermost thoughts to a friend you can trust.
14. Laugh, it's healthy. Don't hold back.
15. Risk showing a little more affection. It's an opportunity to feel good about yourself and to make others feel good at the same time.
16. Be yourself. You don't have to be like anyone else. You're terrific, and people will like you for what you are.

NOTES

1. Richard M. Steers and Daniel N. Braunstein, "A Behaviorally-Based Measure of Manifest Needs in Work Settings," *Journal of Vocational Behavior*, vol. 9 (1976), pp. 251–266.
2. Elizabeth G. French, "Development of a Measure of Complex Motivation," in John W. Atkinson, ed., *Motives in Fantasy, Action, and Society* (Princeton, NJ: Van Nostrand, 1958).

3. H. Harris, *An Experimental Model of the Effectiveness of Project Management Offices*, Master's dissertation, Massachusetts Institute of Technology, 1969.
4. J. B. Lansing and Roger W. Heyns, "Need Affiliation and Frequency of Four Types of Communication," *Journal of Abnormal and Social Psychology*, vol. 58 (1959) pp. 365–372.
5. David C. McClelland, "Inhibited Power Motivation and High Blood Pressure in Men," *Journal of Abnormal Psychology*, vol. 88, (1979), pp. 182–190.
6. McClelland, C. Alexander, and E. Marks, "The Need for Power, Stress, Immune Function and Illness among Male Prisoners, *Journal of Abnormal Psychology*, vol. 91 (1982), pp. 61–70.
7. John B. Jemmott III, *Psychosocial Stress, Social Motives and Diseases Susceptibility*, Doctoral dissertation, Harvard University, 1982.
8. McClelland, *Human Motivation* (Glenview, IL: Scott, Foresman, 1985), p. 366.
9. McClelland *Human Motivation*; McClelland and Richard E. Boyatzis, "The Leadership Motive Pattern and Long-Term Success in Management," *Journal of Applied Psychology*, vol. 67 (1982), pp. 737–743; S. W. Kock, [*Management and motivation*], English summary of a doctoral dissertation presented at the Swedish School of Economics, Helsinki, Finland, 1965; Herbert A. Wainer and Irwin M. Rubin, "Motivation of Research and Development Entrepreneurs, *Journal of Applied Psychology*, vol. 53 (1969) pp. 178–184.
10. Douglas P. Crowne and D. Marlowe, *The Approval Motive* (New York: John Wiley, 1964).
11. Leonard H. Chusmir, "Motivation of Managers: Is Gender a Factor?" *Psychology of Women Quarterly*, vol. 9 (1985), pp. 153–159.

8 Power: Traveling the Road to Leadership Success

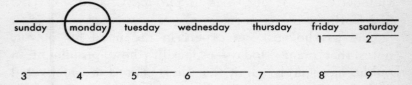

sunday	monday	tuesday	wednesday	thursday	friday	saturday
					1	2
3	4	5	6	7	8	9

Two Types of Power: One Good, One Not So Good

When I was a child I was taught that power was dangerous and evil. I didn't question those teachings, because there were examples all around us of what can happen when very powerful people take control. Hitler was in the middle of his vicious rampage, with help from villains Mussolini and Emperor Hirohito. During the depression, voices of power-hungry ministers preached hatred and anti-Semitism. Most Western thinkers were uncomfortable with the idea of power. Many of us can remember warnings written by Plato, who described the rise of the despot in his society; conclusions by Machiavelli and others that the striving for power was part of man's nature; that unrestrained lust for power corrupts unless tempered by humility, moderation, and restraint. We read of the "robber barons" who founded the great American industrial society, who made themselves and the country among the most powerful in the world. "When nature or habit or both have combined the traits of drunkenness, lust, and lunacy, then you have the perfect specimen of the despotic man . . . Goaded on to frenzy . . . he will look out for any man of property whom he can rob by fraud or violence . . ." (Plato, *The Republic*, Chapter 32 [IX, 572–574]).

One psychologist, an expert in the need for power, notes that people today—especially those prominent in public life—rarely admit that their actions are motivated by a desire for power.[1] They're very careful to avoid using the word, substituting instead such idealistic abstractions as "service," "duty," "responsibility," or "legitimate power." Even the informal but generally accepted definition of the phrase "need for power" avoids negative words when it describes the motive as the desire to have impact or influence over others in order to help them, the organization, or society.

But call it what you want, the need for power is not only part of human nature, it is an essential ingredient in the management of society, in the running of organizations, and in the helping of individuals and groups to rise up from physical, mental, or spiritual poverty.

Need for power is neither evil nor good. It's simply a human drive just like need for achievement, need for affiliation, or any one of hundreds of other needs. It is how need for power is used that determines its acceptability in today's world. Do we use it for personal aggrandizement, to control other human beings just for the thrill of changing their lives to suit our own whims? That's "personalized power." Or do we use it to help other people achieve, to be happy, to cope better with life, or to learn? That's "socialized power." Most of us—even though we don't like to admit it—have a little or a lot of each.

If our need for power consists mostly of personalized power, we're likely to make great dictators or despots. If our drive consists mostly of socialized power, we're likely to make great managers, therapists, teachers, presidents, and a host of other valuable contributors to our society.

Outlets for the Need for Power

If your test results showed that you have a high need for power, how are you likely to behave?

There's no question that people high in need for power act assertively. But is aggressiveness an outlet for power? We learned in the achievement chapter that male college athletes in competitive sports have a very high need for achievement. Often they have a high need for power as well. Older men high in power need also are more apt to be involved in competitive sports, and they get into arguments more often than men low in power need. But the same isn't true of women, who may feel the same urge to be aggressive but hold back, possibly because aggressiveness isn't considered an appropriate sex-role behavior for women.

Both men and women high in power need admit to having aggressive impulses, such as yelling at someone in traffic, breaking dishes, throwing things at someone, or taking towels from a hotel that gave poor service. Most people have become angry and thought about doing those things, but the more mature they are, the less likely it is that they'll act out their aggressions. Social-class values are another moderator of aggressive acts. High-need-for-power working-class men tend to be impulsively aggressive, but that's not true among middle-class men. Overall, people high in the need for power tend to be both aggressive and assertive, but try to act in ways that are socially appropriate, feeling guilt and anxiety when they're not able to control their aggressive tendencies, but comfortable with their assertiveness.[2]

When high-need-for-power people don't control their aggressiveness, they tend to view their antisocial behavior and themselves negatively. The higher the need for power, the more likely it is that individuals will have emotional problems, see themselves as inadequate, be dissatisfied with some aspect of their lives, take too many drugs or drink too much alcohol to relax, and have trouble sleeping.

Not surprisingly, people with high power need enter occupations that put them into a position to influence people. Research shows, for example, that teachers, entertainers, and religious leaders use their public visibility to influence audiences; psychologists and journalists use inside information to influence people; managers use the power of their position to influence subordinates.

Other behavior outlets for high-need-for-power people include the search for prestige by accumulating prestigious material possessions like fancy automobiles, expensive homes and clothing, and a large collection of credit cards. They also call attention to themselves in groups, enjoying the recognition they get. And, finally, they find an outlet for their high need for power in taking high risks, typically either at the gambling table or in the stock market.

A former head of a local construction company rode the roller coaster of success a half-dozen times. Sylvan was a friendly competitor who built middle-priced homes. Sylvan and I often would have lunch together. One day he looked particularly depressed. I wasn't surprised, because business had been slow around town for nearly a year, and most were just holding on until the real estate market improved. "What happened?" I asked, expecting some tale of mortgage or financing problems, and heard both. "I can't believe I did it," Sylvan finally blurted out. "My wife, my controller, my banker . . . everyone told me not to buy that hundred-acre parcel next to my present project. But the landowner was in trouble financially and the price was so cheap I just couldn't resist. I had no cash, so I borrowed on the equity of the business and signed my life away for the rest. Well, I got behind on payments, the bank called the loan, I just met with my attorney this morning, and I've filed for Chapter 11 bankruptcy."

Sylvan was a gambler, and a big-risk-taker at that. Show him a piece of land and a way to control it without cash, and he couldn't resist. A year later Sylvan lost his building business, but within two months he was back in business under a new name. He's on a roll now and one of Florida's most successful home builders. But tomorrow? Who knows?

Characteristics of People With a Strong Need for Power

People who are high in-power-need enjoy jobs where authority and power rest within the position they have. They strive to be leaders, enjoy speaking out assertively, love to coach, influence, teach, or encourage others to achieve. They usually attempt to influence by making suggestions, by giving their opinions and evaluations, and by trying to talk others into things. Because influencing others is important to them, high-power-need people often are verbally fluent, often talkative, sometimes argumentative. High-need-for-power managers feel a personal responsibility for ensuring the success of the organization. They're the first to sacrifice their own self-interest for the welfare of the company; have a strong sense of justice or equity; and are less defensive and more willing to seek expert advice when necessary. They tend to be superior performers, have above-average attendance records, and are rated by others as having good leadership abilities.

For example, a young man named Peter was my research assistant when I taught at the University of Colorado at Denver. A year before, he had been a student in my graduate-level course on individual behavior in organizations and had expressed a great deal of interest in motivation and how it affected people at work. I was scheduled to do a study on motivation needs of the health-care industry, and Peter asked me if he could help out. Peter was president of the M.B.A. Student Association, a deacon in his church, the student representative to the College of Business curriculum committee, and involved in a half-dozen other extracurricular activities. I asked him how he could possibly handle the extra load of being a research assistant on top of all his other activities, including ranking in the upper 10 percent of the M.B.A. class. "No problem," he answered. "You know me and my high need for power. I'm the front man for the M.B.A. Association. The other officers are doing all the work and I check up once in a while. At the curriculum committee I just give input to the faculty; my girlfriend has agreed to put all the data we gather for the health-care study into the computer; and Jerry-the-statistical-genius will do the data analysis for us. I can handle it easily."

Peter did the work and lived up to all his promises and my expectations. I was pleased when Peter walked into my office a couple of years later to say hello and to update me on his career progress. I wasn't surprised to learn that his leadership qualities combined with his high need for impact and influence had already brought him two promotions in the two years since he had started with one of the largest banking firms in Denver. I still hear from Peter occasionally and know he'll be running the bank holding company in another ten years.

High-need-for-power individuals try to control information about themselves. They follow fashions so they'll know the proper clothing to wear and how to effect the proper image. Also, power males get a vicarious power surge by reading magazines such as *Playboy* and *Sports Illustrated*.[3] Regardless of gender, high-need-for-power persons are more likely to be involved in organizations, to like to work, to respect institutional authority, and to be concerned with discipline and self-respect than those with low need for power.[4] Those especially high in socialized power tend to be independent, suspicious of power, and poor performers under stress.

Individuals with a high need for personalized power strive for dominance almost for the sake of dominance. Personal conquest is important to them, and one of the reasons they make poor managers is that they tend to reject organizational responsibilities. According to David McClelland, they're like conquistadors or feudal chieftans; that is, they attempt to inspire their workers to heroic performance but want them to do it for the sake of their leader, not for the organization.

Most of us have known conquistador bosses. If we are lucky they are someone else's boss; if the fates are against us, they run our departments. Ted was the boss of the insurance company credit analysis department when unlucky Eleanor was transferred in. "How did it work out?" I asked her one evening in class. "All I can say," she said, "is that I'm now a full-time M.B.A. student looking to get into marketing."

Unfortunately, a power-oriented manager or professional pays a high price in terms of personal health. McClelland measured need for power among a group of Harvard graduates more than thirty years ago.[5] Twenty years later, in a follow-up study, he found that 58 percent of those rated high in need for power in the earlier study either had high blood pressure or serious signs of potential heart failure.

Need for Power Among U.S. Presidents

As you might guess from the list of one hundred popular power jobs that appear in the Appendix, the job of being President of the United States fulfills a very high level of need for power. Few jobs in the world offer a better chance to have impact and influence. Of course, the job also fulfills a moderate amount of need for achievement, because there are opportunities every day to solve problems. Also, what President wouldn't be forgiven by an admiring American public if he or she showed a little tough competitiveness when it came time to negotiate with other heads of state? Unfortunately for readers of this book who are high in the need for affiliation, that need usually doesn't get fulfilled by being President. Most Presidents (or prime ministers, kings, queens, or dictators) lead very lonely personal lives. There isn't much time left for warm, personal relationships with family and close friends, although they're always surrounded by people.

Being President is no different from any other job in respect to job happiness. Some Presidents had a very good motivational match for their job and others had a poor match. Because we all subscribe to our own personal political point of view, I won't try to make judgments on whether the Presidents with a good match were especially successful or whether those with a bad match were especially ineffective in office. But because each differed in his motivational needs, each brought to the office a different personality and probably a different set of behaviors and responses.

David Winter, a colleague of David McClelland and an acknowledged expert in the field of need for power, did a fascinating study of Presidents and presidential candidates in which he examined inauguration speeches or other verbal and written material, including press conference transcripts and announcement-of-candidacy speeches, to determine their needs for power, achievement and affiliation.[6]

In the 1976 presidential campaign, winner Jimmy Carter's dominant need was for achievement, consistent with his engineering and entrepreneurial background. Winter suggested that Carter exhibited many achievement-oriented behaviors, such as being a good negotiator who took moderate risks (Camp David accords and the Iranian hostage negotiations); a desire for personal responsibility, which unfortunately sometimes manifested itself in an excessive concern with details; and a strong concern for excellence, to lead the "best transition" in history. Gerald Ford, who preceded Jimmy Carter, was high in the need for affiliation. Seen as a friendly, compliant man who listened to the counsel of his advisers, Ford pardoned Richard Nixon out of sympathy, he said, because "he had suffered enough." Winter pointed out that Ford's low need-for-power score was probably confirmed by what Winter described as an "almost reckless disregard for the political and judicial consequences." Ronald Reagan, in 1976, showed a high level of need for both achievement and power, similar to Franklin D. Roosevelt when he first took office. In a conversation with motivation researcher Abigail Stewart, Winter contended that both Reagan and Roosevelt had similar styles and even similar rhetoric, both emphasizing that "the nation's heritage is threatened by crisis . . . both emphasiz[ing] that specific programs aren't enough; both call[ing] for a new philosophy of government."[7] Even though their political views were different, their needs, behavior, and strategies were strikingly similar.

Winter measured the needs of most of the unsuccessful 1976 candidates as well and found that Fred Harris, Ellen McCormack, George Wallace, Henry Jackson, and Morris Udall were all high in need for power and were "great crusaders in the mold of Woodrow Wilson, who showed the same motive pattern." Other Democratic candidates and their dominant need included Birch Bayh (moderate, balanced); Lloyd Bentsen (high achievement and affiliation); Frank Church (high achievement); Hubert Humphrey (high achievement and affiliation); Terry Sanford (high achievement and power); Milton Shapp (high achievement); and Sargent Shriver (high affiliation). Nelson Rockefeller, the other unsuccessful Republican candidate, was high in affiliation need.

Past Presidents, other than those mentioned, were tested for motivation needs as well. Teddy Roosevelt and Jack Kennedy had the two highest needs for power of any U.S. Presidents since the turn of the century. Harry Truman's dominant need also was power, and quite high; Richard Nixon, surprisingly to some, had a dominant need for achievement, as did Lyndon Johnson and Herbert Hoover, although Hoover's was very low compared to the other two. Dwight Eisenhower, William Taft, Warren Harding, and Calvin Coolidge all had dominant needs for power, but all were relatively low compared to some of the others.

Sex Differences in Need for Power

Most studies of sex differences show women in general to be lower than or at best comparable to men in the need for power. Even when the drives are the same, women tend to satisfy their need in ways that are socially accept-able. For example, men associate power with leadership at work or in athletics. But until recently, leadership in business and public organizations was off-limits to women. Teaching was one of the few "sex-appropriate" occupations for women in which power could be exercised. Therefore, a woman's need for power was confined to her handling of socially accepted male-female relationships. In these situa-tions, studies showed that women demonstrated their higher power motivations by seeking enduring relationships with men in order to yield personal power and control over them.

Times are changing, and so are women. Today, women managers have a higher need for socialized and corporate power (the desirable type) than do men managers. Their need for personalized power (the less desirable type) is the same as male managers'.

A woman I recently met named Ursula was a housewife for the first fifteen years of her marriage. While bringing up her children she was a volunteer for the League of Women Voters, dedicating herself to making change in her community. At a dinner party not too long ago, she told me that she loved what she did, but now at thirty-seven years of age and recently divorced, she wants a paid career and hopes to be director of a social service agency. "I need to make a decent living, now that I'm on my own," she related, "but at the same time I have to do something that can help people. I've been a mother and a wife all my life and helping is what I'm really good at."

As time passes, managers are likely to see similar signs among their female nonmanagement employees. But, thus, far, although individual women may possess a strong need for power, most women don't.

Sex differences in need for power go far beyond the amount of drive each gender is likely to have. Even when men and women have the same amount of need for power, they express that concern differently, so their behavior is different as well. Here are some of those behavioral differences:

In a major research project on sex differences in power motives conducted during the mid-1970s, men high in power motivation were found more likely to recall dreams, to have trouble sleeping, to check on home security, to be concerned with good will, and to share more information about their sex lives than men low in power need. High-need-for-power women, however, tended to be more concerned about diet, appearance, and clothes, and to have more credit cards. They drank more, volunteered to donate body parts after death, and had more unpleasant dreams than women low in need for power.[8] Women, therefore, tend to see themselves as a valuable resource, so they're concerned about their bodies more than are high-power-need men. It is through this valuable resource that women can achieve influence and impact. Men, the researcher contended, find strength and power in their emotional assertiveness, rather than in their bodies.

High-need-for-power women do much better in relationships than high-need-for-power men. It's possible that female sex-role inhibitions soften a woman's aggressive responses when she's angry or frustrated. More likely, though, women's socialization has taught them greater relationship skills and instilled a value for relationships that most men don't possess. Power motivation generally predicts difficulties in relationships with the opposite sex, break-up of relationships, and divorce, but this applies to men only.[9] Men, unfortunately, often use their intimate relationships as an arena for achieving the power they may not be able to get elsewhere. They'll be just as aggressive at home as they are at work. Although women may start relationships to satisfy their need for power, they rarely use the relationship as a battleground, choosing to exercise their more assertive behavior outside of the home.

While high-need-for-power men are more likely to express their needs by fighting, drinking, gambling, or trying to exploit women sexually, women express their power drive in more socially responsible ways. They look after members of their family who need help and care; they become therapists, hold public office; or remain "big sisters" to a younger brother or sister, even when both have been adults for many decades.

Jobs that Fulfill the Need for Power

You've read about all the great jobs that fulfill a high need for power—those held by Presidents, presidential candidates, chief executive officers, managers, high-powered professionals, and so forth. That doesn't mean that all the people who hold those jobs are happy in them. In the past, several U.S. Presidents who did a poor job running the country were found to be mismatched motivationally. Did they do a poor job because they were unhappy and unfilled in their work? Or did they do a poor job because they didn't possess the necessary skills? The answer will never be known, although some Americans may have strong personal opinions.

Most of us who have a high need for power don't occupy such lofty positions as heads of government. But the jobs we hold are also important—either to us or to the organizations for which we work. And sometimes those jobs are not suited to our high need for power.

If you're one of the fifty-four million American workers who are unhappy with their job, and if you have a high need for power, check the list in the Appendix to see if your present occupation or job is listed. Chances are your job is not on the list. In that case it may be time for you to think either about changing jobs or planning some action to get more satisfaction from your work.

If your job is on the list of one hundred jobs likely to fulfill the need for power, and you're still unhappy at work, there may be reasons other than fulfillment of motivation needs for the dissatisfaction. In that case, continue reading on to the end of the chapter for many ideas about how to make your present job more satisfying.

When you examine the list of one hundred power jobs, you'll quickly see that not all are top-level positions. Many are good-paying, satisfying, "normal" jobs, suitable for the majority of Americans who enjoy having influence over others and who find that making an impact on society, on strangers, on their fellow workers, on their company, or on their community is important to them.

How to Be Happier at Work Without Changing Jobs

Can you imagine how some President of the United States might have felt after being elected and waking up one morning to the realization that he hated his job? That he felt unfulfilled, frustrated, and dissatisfied? Don't laugh. Historians have been very unkind to a few U.S. Presidents who were smart enough to know how to do a good job but nevertheless were very poor leaders. Once elected President, it's not likely that anyone will resign just because they're unhappy in the job. All our Presidents—good and bad—were tough enough to stick it out, assuming of course, that they weren't forced out. But in the real world of employment, we do have choices. Hundreds, perhaps thousands, of presidents of large companies have decided to quit, to retire early, or to hand the reins over to someone else because they were unhappy at work. At lower levels and among professionals in every possible field, women and men quit every day to find something more fulfilling.

But millions of others stick it out. They stay with their job and do everything they can to make it work, to make it a little happier. If you're one of them, the rest of this chapter is written just for you.

Things You Can Do at Work to Help Fulfill Your Need for Power

1. Become a supervisor or manager. That's the best opportunity for having influence and impact on others.
2. Make professional presentations at work or at conferences.
3. Act as the union shop steward.
4. Join a group. Make yourself known and build alliances.
5. Accept offers for training and development workshops in highly specialized areas where you can become an expert. Expertise is an excellent source of power.
6. Volunteer for your company's speakers' bureau to give speeches at local organizations.
7. Be a spokesperson for your company at school activities.
8. Represent your company and join a community organization such as a Rotary Club or Kiwanis.
10. Decorate your office to make it more attractive and homelike. Hang some artwork on the wall.
11. Make sure the information in your department flows through your desk before going "upstairs."
12. Use the company grapevine to obtain and disperse important information.

13. Become part of the good old boys' or good old girls' network.
14. Don't eat lunch at your desk. Always ask one of your colleagues to join you for lunch and go out together.

Things Your Manager Can Do at Work to Help Fulfill Your Need for Power

1. Let you head special task forces or committees.
2. Assign you the job of training new or current workers.
3. Make periodic reports directly available to you rather than to her- or himself.
4. Give you a budget to take customers or other workers out for lunch.
5. Appoint you to help out in the company's employee assistance program.
6. Send you to national or regional conferences.
7. Reimburse you for tuition expenses to take management courses at your local university.
8. Appoint you to represent your department by writing news releases for your company employee newspaper.
9. Ask you to be in charge of employee welfare.
10. Appoint you team leader of a workers' committee to suggest ways to improve production quality.
11. Move your office to a more visible or central location.
12. Redecorate your office.
13. Give you a title.
14. Recognize your value to the firm in front of other workers.

Things You Can Do at Home to Fulfill Your Need for Power

1. Buy a foreign car or a convertible the next time you're ready to trade in or sell your old car.
2. Carry all your credit cards in your wallet. If you don't have enough to fill a large clear plastic holder, apply for some more cards.
3. Buy a very large color TV set if you can afford it.
4. Teach a course at the local community college in your area of expertise.
5. Be a chaperon or adult counselor for a high school or college fraternity or sorority.
6. Join and become active in any charitable organization.
7. Coach a Little League or recreation department sports team.
8. Become a Scout leader.
9. Become a member of the board of your church or temple.
10. Teach Sunday school.
11. Get an M.B.A. degree.
12. Join a debating society.
13. Write articles or guest columns for your local newspaper.
14. Go to an expert and have your "colors" done. Find out which colors are best for your look.
15. Spend the extra money for good-quality clothing if you can afford it. You'll look better, and you'll feel better.
16. Subscribe to a fashion magazine, and read it regularly. Remember that there are fashion magazines for men as well as for women.
17. Be a "Big Brother" or "Big Sister."

18. Buy a dog. Teach it new tricks. It will respect and obey you—perhaps even love you—even if you're not the nicest person in the world to live with.
19. Join the local amateur theater group.

NOTES

1. David G. Winter, *The Power Motive* (New York: The Free Press, 1973).
2. David C. McClelland, *Human Motivation* (Glenview, IL: Scott, Foresman, 1985).
3. Winter, *The Power Motive*.
4. Abigail J. Stewart, ed., *Motivation and Society* (San Francisco: Jossey-Bass, 1985).
5. McClelland "Sources of Stress in the Drive for Power," in George Serban, ed., *Psychopathology of Human Adaptation* (New York: Plenum Press, 1976).
6. Winter and Stewart, "Content Analysis as a Method of Studying Political Leaders," in M. G. Hermann, ed., *A Psychological Examination of Political Leaders* (New York: The Free Press, 1977); R. E. Donley and Winter, "Measuring the Motives of Public Officials at a Distance: An Exploratory Study of American Presidents," *Behavioral Science*, vol. 15 (1970), pp. 227–236.
7. Stewart, *Motivation and Society*, p. 251.
8. McClelland, *Power: The Inner Experience* (New York: Irvington, 1975).
9. Abigail J. Stewart and Z. Rubin, "The Power Motive in the Dating Couple," *Journal of Personality and Social Psychology*, Vol. 34 (1974), pp. 304–309; Joseph Veroff and S. Feld, *Marriage and Work in America: A Study of Motives and Roles* (New York: Van Nostrand Reinhold, 1970); David Winter, Abigail J. Stewart, and David C. McClelland, "Husband's Motives and Wife's Career Level," *Journal of Personality and Social Psychology*, vol. 35 (1977), pp. 159–166.

9 Other Need Profiles: Not As Common But Still Very Important

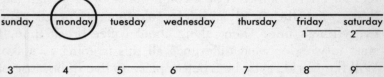

sunday monday tuesday wednesday thursday friday saturday
                                                1   2

3   4   5   6   7   8   9

The three preceding chapters each dealt with one of three dominant needs: achievement, affiliation, and power. Most American jobs—but not all—fulfill one of the needs to a greater extent than any of the others. But many fulfill relatively equal amounts of two or even all three needs. For that reason, this chapter will cover the last four of the seven different need profiles discussed in Chapter 2. Those four motivation need profiles are:

- Balance of all three needs
- Needs for achievement and power
- Needs for achievement and affiliation
- Needs for affiliation and power

What happens when a person has two or three dominant needs and his or her job fulfills mostly one? The one that's fulfilled by the job is okay, but the others left unattended cause frustration, or at least a sense of something unknown missing, leaving the person unsatisfied, vaguely discontent, wondering what's missing.

For example, Sid felt very neutral about his job. He could take it or leave it. "Sometimes I feel great at work," he told us one day in his M.B.A. class. "When I sit down at the drafting table and pick up my architectural tools, I feel an energy surge. For a couple of hours I design and draw what the head architect told me he needs, and everything's fine. Then, along about coffee-break time, I start to wonder what difference all this is going to make. Will the world really be a better place to live in because of the office layout I'm doing for the twenty-seventh floor of a thirty-story building? Who'll ever know that the west wing of the floor was my creation? And, worse yet, who cares?" Sid, as you probably guessed, had both a high need for achievement and a high need for power. His need for achievement was fulfilled by the problem-solving challenge of his entry-level architectural job, and by his careful, exacting craftsmanship. But not his need for power. His job gave him no opportunity to have impact on anyone he could identify, and no chance to influence the client or other workers in the firm.

People like Sid have a personal problem. They have two or three strong needs but a job that leaves one or more unsatisfied. Sometimes they're able to satisfy the unfulfilled need outside of work, or they're able to modify their jobs a little to help make them more meaningful. Chapters 6, 7, and 8 listed many suggestions to help fulfill the needs for achievement, affiliation, and power.

But what happens when the reverse is true—when a job fulfills more needs than a person has? For example, if a job fulfills all three needs and the person in the job has a high need for one but doesn't care about the other two, who's affected? In that case, the company as well as the individual has a problem. The portion of the job that fulfills the worker's dominant need likely will get attended to first, leaving the portions that fulfill unneeded motives worked on last, if at all. We all know people who procrastinate, who never seem to get "important" things done. It's like sitting down at the dinner table and being handed a dinner plate containing some of your favorite sliced turkey and stuffing, but also a pile of limp spinach. The turkey probably will be gobbled up immediately because it satisfies your visual and taste needs. But if you're like the majority of people who have no desire to eat spinach, it may hang around uneaten or stabbed to death by the prongs of the fork. Some people, of course, love spinach— perhaps as much or more than turkey. For them, the entire dinner will be wonderful. The same is true at work. Unfortunately, though, when a portion of the job is left undone too often, or is done poorly, the organization may take action against the individual.

People in jobs that fulfill either too many or too few of their needs ought to consider the same two possibilities we discussed earlier in this book. They ought to either change jobs or try to fulfill their missing needs in other ways.

Jobs That Fulfill a Balance of Needs

Many jobs fulfill a reasonable amount of all three needs. Very few, however, fulfill a very high level of all three. When a person has a job that involves a combination of supervision and hands-on work, and when that job takes place in close proximity to others, all three needs will probably be fulfilled. Low-level supervisors often have a dual responsibility because they need to look after just a few workers and may still have time to do some of the technical or skilled work themselves. In a sense they're almost the same as the others, but have the added responsibility of "being in charge."

For example, Ben is a twenty-eight-year old carpentry supervisor on a housing project. He usually works with four other carpenters who specialize in doing a variety of work, ranging from putting up the wooden forms for pouring concrete foundations to setting roof trusses or erecting room partitions. The five work as a team. Ben and the others are buddies. They like working together, but Ben has been on the job longer than his fellow carpenters, and they look up to him as a team leader. Ben's job fulfills all three of his needs and he's one of the happiest individuals I've known. He works hard and plays hard, and enjoys both.

In the Appendix, you'll find the list of jobs that fulfill a balance of needs. Note that each one involves all three important criteria. Each provides the opportunity for some hands-on work that may not be extraordinarily skilled but does involve some challenge or some technical proficiency (fulfills need for achievement). Each also involves having impact or influence over others. This does not necessarily mean that people in such jobs are managers or bosses. Airline flight attendants, for example, can affect a passenger's trip by the quality of service given; receptionists may choose to be helpful or not to people asking for help (which fulfills the need for power).

Finally, all jobs that fulfill a balance of needs involve the individual job holder with other people, either as close-by fellow workers or as customers or clients (which fulfills the need for affiliation). When any aspect of those three criteria are missing from the job, the job will not be satisfying to the balanced-need individual.

Jobs That Fulfill Needs for Achievement and Power

Although not as common as jobs fulfilling a balance of all three needs, there are many occupations and positions that fulfill a relatively equal amount of achievement and power. Generally, these are highly skilled tasks often involving technical ability used to influence others to produce a product or service that has significant impact on the lives of others. In contrast to the more moderate, more balanced personality, the need-for-achievement-and-power person often is strongly driven by his or her needs. Many of my newspaper consulting jobs have brought me into contact with persons high in both needs.

A few years ago, I was hired by a newspaper chain to lower its level of turnover on the job. Some of their brightest young people stayed for a year or two and then left, despite the fact that salaries paid at the newspapers were very competitive. Jill was city editor of one of the smaller papers, and when I interviewed her, I discovered the first clue that the newspapers were doing a poor job matching the needs of their workers to their jobs. Jill told me she sometimes felt like a misfit. "When I got my journalism degree," she said, "I wanted to be an investigative reporter, and I was thrilled when the paper hired me. I was an idealist and an activist in college, and now I had a chance to do something really meaningful. After five years, I did such a good job they promoted me to city editor. I like telling the reporters what to do and how to do it. I'm very creative and can usually help them a lot. But the job is so involved with details and keeping track of dozens of story leads that I find part of what I do a waste of time."

Jobs That Fulfill Needs for Achievement and Affiliation

Many individuals have relatively high needs for achievement and affiliation. There are very few jobs that fulfill both these needs, however, and this potential mismatch may present problems at work. Because it's so difficult to find jobs that are a good natural match for this combination, workers may have to get their satisfaction through other people with whom they work.

For example, we know that they perform best at very difficult jobs when their bosses or coworkers give them approval and tell them how pleased they are with the results. Also, managers sometimes have problems supervising subordinates of the opposite sex. That's especially true of female managers, who may not be accepted by all male workers. But the reverse is true for managers when their workers are of the opposite sex and have high needs for achievement and affiliation. Results of several studies suggest that male workers try much harder to please a female boss, especially when she is present watching the males' performance.[1] The reverse is probably true as well. Workers high in achievement and affiliation needs perform much better in highly competitive situations with same-sex competitors than those competing against opposite-sex peers.

Jobs That Fulfill Needs for Affiliation and Power

In some cultures, especially in countries such as Mexico and Italy, high needs for power and affiliation often are found in the same individuals.[2] Families are very paternalistic, and so are many of the firms run by families. The close affiliative tie of the family is encouraged and maintained in the firm, which commonly uses its strong sense of power and competitiveness to pit the family firm against outsiders. Research in those countries and among U.S. immigrants of the same groups found that people within the closely knit family or firm often look to highly inspirational figures for their own strength, find security in having personal ties with the leaders, and commonly see the "nonfamily" individual as a threat.

While this need combination can work successfully in a paternalistic family firm, it rarely works well in the more typical U.S. company owned by strangers or publicly owned. In that case, managers with a high need for affiliation often make decisions based on personal judgments of individuals, leading to accusations of unfairness, poor morale, and lower productivity. The American business ethic—quite different from that of some other cultural groups—encourages separation of personal feelings and business decisions.

Very few jobs in this country are designed to satisfy both the need for affiliation and the need for power. As you can see from the list in the Appendix, jobs that satisfy both are extremely rare. Individuals high in both needs, howevers, are not so rare. There are hundreds of thousands—perhaps even millions—of Americans who have a strong desire to belong or to be loved, and yet want to have impact and influence on others. The problem is not in having those needs; it's in getting them both satisfied at work. As a general rule, people high in both affiliation and power needs ought to look at ways to satisfy those needs outside their jobs. They can help themselves be happier at work by rechecking the suggestions at the end of chapters 7 and 8.

NOTES

1. U. J. Jopt, as cited in Heinz Heckhausen, *Motivation und Handeln [Motivation and Action]* (New York: Springer-Verlag, 1980); John W. Atkinson and P. O'Connor, "Neglected Factors in Studies of Achievement-oriented Performance: Social Approval as an Incentive and Performance Decrement," in Atkinson and N. T. Feather, eds. *A Theory of Achievement Motivation* (New York: John Wiley, 1966).
2. David C. McClelland, *Human Motivation* (Glenview, IL: Scott, Foresman, 1985).

Appendix

A Complete List of Jobs That Fulfill Each of the Seven Motivation Profiles

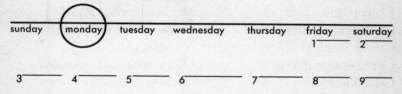

sunday monday tuesday wednesday thursday friday saturday

1   2

3   4   5   6   7   8   9

Jobs That Fulfill the Need for Achievement

Accountant, tax
Accounting clerk
Acupuncturist
Answering service operator

Appliance servicer
Architect
Art director
Artist

Assistant buyer
Auditor, external
Baker
Billing typist
Biochemist
Biologist
Blue-collar worker (skilled)
Bookbinder
Bookkeeper
Botanist
Business investor
Butcher
Buyer (most types)
Cashier
Chemist
Chief engineer
Child psychologist
Chiropractor
Civil service clerk
Clerks (high skill, technical)
Congressional aide
Cook/chef
Counter clerk
Craftsperson, skilled
Decorator
Dentist (most types)
Doctor (most types)
Drafter
Electrician
Engineer (most types)
Engraver
Entrepreneur
Fashion consultant
Freight traffic agent
Fund-raiser

Home economist
Houseworker
Hypnotherapist
Industrial designer
Inspector
Insurance agent
Installer, equipment
Instrument maker
Interior designer/decorator
Jeweler
Lawyer (most types)
Leasing agent
Legal secretary
Machine operator
Maintenance supervisor
Make-up artist
Mechanic
Medical technologist
Metalsmith (any type)
Nutritionist
Office machine operator
Owner, business
Painter
Personal shopper
Pharmacist
Photojournalist
Photographer
Physicist
Plumber
Printer
Programmer, business
Psychologist, nonclinical
Radio station operator
Real estate broker
Repairer (all types)

Researcher
Sales agent
Sales representatives (most types)
Scientist
Secretary, general
Security guard
Set designer
Software technician
Stenographer
Tailor
Tax preparer

Technician
Telemarketing rep
Telephone operator
Telephone solicitor
Teller
Tester
Travel agent
TV installer
Typist
Wine steward
X-ray technician

Jobs That Fulfill the Need for Affiliation

Advertising space clerk
Ambulance attendant
Animal caretaker
Assembler, production
Assistant physician
Automobile wrecker
Bartender
Bellhop
Caddie
Cafeteria worker
Campground caretaker
Car hop
Cashier, box office
Catalog librarian
Cemetery worker
Christmas tree farm worker
Clerk (low skill)
Clubhouse attendant

Coat/hat checker
Coin machine operator
Collator
Cook helper
Custodian
Day care center worker
Deliverer (all types)
Dishwasher
Dog pound attendant
Doll repairer
Doorkeeper
Dresser
Equipment inventory clerk
Exerciser
Exterminator
Extra (acting)
Fast food cashier
Final inspector

Fingerprint classifier
Fire eater
Fountain server
Funeral attendant
Fur cleaner
Gambling dealer
Garbage/trash collector
Garment inspector
Gas station attendant
Grip (theater)
Helper, manufacturing
Hospital emergency
   medical attendant
Hospital ward attendant
Host/hostess
Housecleaner
Janitor
Key cutter
Kitchen helper
Laboratory assistant
Laborer (any type)
Licensed practical nurse
Machine helper
Manicurist
Masseur/masseuse
Mechanic helper
Messenger
Military crewmember
Mover
Nurse, general duty
Nurse, doctor's office
Nurse's aide
Order filler
Parking enforcement officer

Parking lot attendant
Parking meter coin collector
Personal attendant
Picket, labor union
Police officer, ID and
   records
Porter
Press clippings clerk
Produce clerk
Proofreader
Psychiatric aide
Psychic reader
Rental clerk
Sales attendant, self-service
Schedule coordinator
Scorer, sports events
Scuba diver
Self-service laundry
   attendant
Service representative
Ski patroller
Snow shoveler
Sorter
Steward/stewardess
Street cleaner
Supermarket bagger
Ticket seller
Tobacco checkout clerk
Tree planter
Upholsterer
Usher
Waiter/waitress
Warehouse checker

Jobs That Fulfill the Need for Power

Accompanist, music
Accountant executive
Accountant, general
Actor/actress
Administrative assistant
Administrative officer
Administrator
Agent (any type)
Aide to manager
Airline pilot, copilot
Allergist, M.D.
Ambulance driver
Analyst (any type)
Announcer
Appraiser, real estate
Armored car driver
Astrologer
Athlete, professional
Athletic trainer
Auditor, internal
Auditor, tax
Branch manager
Chairman of the board
Checker
Chief executive officer
Choreographer
Claims adjuster
Clergyman
Coach, sports
Consultant
Controller
Counselor

Credit analyst
Credit manager
Dancer
Dean
Department head
Detective
Director
Dispatcher
District attorney
Elevator operator
Entertainer
Executive
Executive editor
Executive secretary
Field representative
Fire chief
Firefighter
General manager
Head nurse
Hospital administrator
Instructor
Investigator
Jockey
Judge
Lawyer, criminal
Librarian (most types)
Loan officer
Manager
Managing editor
Middle manager
Military officer
Musician, instrumental

Nurse supervisor
Operations officer
Plant superintendent
Police
Postmaster
President
Principal
Professor, college
Program director
Project manager
Publisher (non-owner)
Psychiatrist
Psychologist, clinical
Quality engineer
Radio/TV announcer
Racer, auto
Recruiter
Reporter
Reservations and ticketing
    clerk

Sales manager
Security guard
Security officer
Social worker
Stockbroker
Superintendent (any type)
Supervisor (mid–high
    level)
Talent agent
Taxi driver
Teacher
Test driver
Therapist
Treasurer
Truck/bus driver
Trust officer
Undercover agent
Vice-president

Jobs That Fulfill a Balance of Needs

Airline flight attendant
Airline gate agent
Animal shelter clerk
Appraiser
Automobile repossessor
Bailiff
Bibliographer
Bouncer
Car wash attendant
Card player
Cargo agent

Claims collector
Clerk (moderately skilled)
Clerk typist
Commercial designer
Comparison shopper
Conductor
Correction officer
Court officer
Customer service
    representative
Dispatch clerk

Dog licenser
Driver helper
Election clerk
Escort
Escrow officer
Estimator
Expediter
Film editor
Film rental clerk
Fire captain/lieutenant
Fire ranger
Foreman/forewoman
Gate attendant
Golf course starter
Guard (all types)
Guide
Helper, electrician
Host/hostess
Insurance collector
Liaison representative
Library assistant
Lifeguard
Loan application closer
Loan interviewer
Mail carrier
Material planner
Medical assistant
Medical records technician
Messenger
Meter Reader (gas/electric)
Model
Monitor
Museum attendant
Nurse midwife
Observer

Packaging engineer
Page
Park aide
Passenger agent
Paymaster
Personal property assessor
Personnel scheduler
Phone book deliverer
Postal clerk
Programmer, information
  systems
Prompter
Receptionist
Reducing salon attendant
Referral information aide
Registration clerk
Reservations agent
Safety inspector
Screenwriter
Security guard
Service representative
Sexton
Shipping order clerk
Ski lift operator
Skip tracer
Social services aide
Stock clerk
Store detective
Story analyst
Supervisor (low level)
Surveyor helper
Tax searcher
Taxi cab starter
Telephone ad taker
Telephone order clerk

Tennis court attendant
Ticket agent
Timekeeper
Title examiner
Traffic clerk
Understudy (theater)

Underwriting analyst
Utility worker
Veterinary meat/poultry
    inspector
X-ray file clerk

Jobs That Fulfill the Needs for Achievement and Power

Acquisitions editor
Ambassador
Anthropologist
Apartment house manager
Astronomer
Bell captain
Book editor
Butler
Chief clerk
Comedy writer
Copywriter
Costumer
Creative director
Day care director
Economist
Engineering analyst
Field service representative
Geographer
Headwaiter/headwaitress
Historian
Humorist
Lobbyist
Lyricist

Manager, internal security
Market research analyst
Mathematician
Motel manager
News analyst
Newspaper city editor
Newspaper metro editor
Newspaper columnist
Newspaper critic
Newspaper editorial writer
Operations research analyst
Orchestrator
Playwright
Poet
Police department
    secretary
Political scientist
Producer-director
Psychometrist
Public relations practitioner
Reservations manager
Restaurant maître d'hôtel
Retail department manager

Section head
Statistician
Supervisor (low level)

Usher, head
Writer, prose

Jobs That Fulfill the Needs for Achievement and Affiliation (Rare)

Abstract checker
Accounting clerk
Adding machine operator
Assembler (skilled)
Brokerage clerk
Dental assistant
Electrologist
Food and beverage checker

Furniture restorer
Insurance checker
Machine operator (factory)
Make-up artist
Nurse anesthetist
Offset press operator
Payroll clerk

Jobs That Fulfill the Needs for Affiliation and Power (Very Rare)

Dog catcher/warden
Drive-in theater attendant
Humane officer

Vending machine coin
   collector